Greek Cookbook

Traditional Greek Recipes Made Easy

www.grizzlypublishing.com

Table of Contents

Introduction

I want to thank you for purchasing this book, 'Greek Cookbook: Traditional Greek Recipes Made Easy.'

Greek cuisine has a very rich culinary tradition spanning several millennia that permeates the country up to this day. From the Hellenistic and the Roman periods, to the Byzantium and Ottoman Empires, Greek cuisine was shaped by history more than any other cuisine in the entire world.

Greek Cuisine can be broken down into its most basic elements which it was founded on, known as the "Mediterranean Triad," this term refers to wheat, olive oil, and wine. Olive oil, produced from the trees that is abundant throughout the region, is prominent in most dishes, lending a very distinct taste that characterized Greek food. Wheat is the staple grain in Greece (although barley is also grown and consumed). Wine, since the spread of grapes in the Mediterranean, is as much an integral part of their culture as it is in their cuisine.

Greek cookery makes use of a myriad of flavorings and spices, some of which are basil, thyme, oregano, mint, dill just to name a few. Since spices are locally grown throughout the region, they are never in short supply.

Season and geography account for the diversity of Greek cuisine. Due to having terrain that is more suitable to breeding sheep and goats, beef dishes are far less common in Greece. Fish dishes, on the other hand, are quite prominent among the coastal areas and the island communities.

If you are looking for a cookbook that will help bolster your skills in cooking Greek food, or you're simply looking to augment your repertoire of Greek recipes, then this is the right book for you. The recipes presented within these pages will help you create a wide array of traditional Greek dishes, not just suitable for special occasions but for everyday meals as well. From dinner parties to just plain dinner, from breakfast to lunch, you will find what your taste buds are craving for. The recipes are tried and tested, and they are easy to understand and simple enough even for a novice cook to follow. The key is to start with great and fresh ingredients, follow the recipe, taste as you cook, and before you know it you are putting out scrumptious Greek dishes that are flavorful and authentic.

Chapter One: Greek Breakfast Recipes

Kagianas (Greek Style Scrambled Eggs with Cherry Tomatoes and Feta)

Serves: 1

Ingredients:

- 2 medium-large eggs
- 10 ounces of cherry tomatoes sliced in half (2 cups)
- 2 tablespoons olive/vegetable oil
- 1-2 teaspoons dried oregano
- 1 small onion chopped
- 1 garlic clove minced
- 1 tablespoon tomato paste mixed with 2-3 tablespoons water
- 1 tablespoon crumbled feta
- 1 teaspoon fresh mint
- salt and pepper to taste

Method:

1. Heat the oil in a medium skillet on a low-medium fire, sauté onion until smooth, add the minced garlic and sauté for about 1 minute.
2. Add the tomatoes and sauté for another 2 minutes.
3. In a little bowl, blend the tomato paste with 2-3 tablespoons water. It ought to be solid and creamy. Add it to the skillet and simmer for about 5-7 minutes until tomatoes wilt.
4. Whisk the eggs in a little bowl and put into skillet, increase the heat and mix quickly but carefully not smashing the tomatoes, heat for approximately 2 minutes until eggs thicken.

5. Remove from skillet, serve on dish. Add salt and pepper to your liking.
6. Add a dash of crumbled feta, dried mint and oregano.

Spanakopita (Greek Spinach and Feta Pie)

Serves: 4-5

Ingredients:

- 12 phyllo sheets
- 10-12 ounces crumbled and grated feta
- 3 medium-large eggs
- 3 tablespoons chopped parsley
- 2 tablespoons olive oil plus more for brushing the phyllo
- 2 tablespoons chopped dill
- 1-pound frozen spinach (defrosted)
- 1 onion finely chopped or 3-4 spring onions chopped (use only the white parts)
- 1/4 cup chopped fresh mint (or dry)
- 1/4 teaspoon nutmeg
- 1 teaspoon sugar

Method:

1. Preheat oven at 350 degrees Fahrenheit (180 Celsius)
2. Heat a small-medium pan and add one tablespoon of olive oil, sauté the onions until smooth.
3. Dry the spinach of any excess water and add it to the pan, sauté with onion for about 2 minutes.
4. Add the natural herbs, nutmeg and sugar and sauté for 2-3 minutes more. Set it aside and allow it to cool.
5. Mince half of the feta and crumble the others.
6. In a little bowl, whisk the egg and add the feta to it.
7. Add the egg mix to the spinach and add another tablespoon of olive oil. Mix thoroughly.
8. Brush a skillet that is approximately 10 X 15 ins with olive oil.
9. Place a sheet of phyllo in the skillet and brush it with olive oil. Do it again with 5 more phyllo sheets.

10. Spread on the spinach blend evenly.
11. Cover with 6 more phyllo sheets and brush each one with olive oil. Slice the phyllo hanging on the skillet or roll it in.
12. Score the top with a blade (do not slice completely, just through the top of the phyllo bed sheets) for approximately 10-12 pieces.
13. 1Bake for approximately 40 minutes until phyllo is turns into golden brown.
14. Remove from the oven and allow the pita to cool.
15. Cut to your liking and serve while hot.

Eliopsomo (Whole Wheat Olive and Feta Cheese Bread)

Serves: 4-6

Ingredients:

- 2 cups (250 gr) all-purpose flour
- 2 cups (250 gr) whole-wheat flour
- 2 teaspoons (7 gr) instant dry yeast
- 2-3 tablespoons oregano
- 1 cup warm water
- 1 tablespoon salt
- 1/4 cup olive oil
- 1/2 cup chopped olives
- 1/2 cup (60 gr) crumbled feta cheese

Method:

1. In a big bowl, mix the yeast with the flour and then add water.
2. Add the salt and essential olive oil and blend well.
3. Now put the dough on the floured surface and begin kneading. Stretch out the dough and then move it back. Do this a couple of times until the dough is elastic and soft, about 7-10 minutes.
4. Roll in a ball and cover with plastic sheet and place it in a bowl. Cover it with a towel and allow it sit someplace warm for approximately an hour.
5. Take the ball and divide it into 2. Stretch out the ball so you have an extended piece of dough. Pour about fifty percent of the olives, fifty percent of the feta and fifty percent of the oregano. Form again in a ball ensuring all the olives are tucked inside.
6. Repeat this process the other dough.

7. Put both balls on the pan, flattening them a little bit and let them sit for approximately 30 minutes
8. Preheat your oven to 425 F (220 C).
9. Sprinkle some flour on of the dough and make a little cut.
10. Bake for approximately 30 minutes.
11. Because of the olives and feta, this bread is a little moist; so, allow it cool down a little before serving, or it could break apart.

Sfougato (Rhodes Quiche Greek Style Omelette)

Serves: 3-4

Ingredients:

- 4 medium-large eggs
- 2 small zucchinis (diced)
- 1 tablespoon parsley (diced)
- 1 garlic clove (pressed, you can add more to your liking)
- 1-2 sprigs thyme
- ½ pound ground beef
- ½ cup chicken broth
- ½ onion (diced)
- ½ teaspoon oregano
- ¼ cup crumbled feta cheese, plus extra for garnish
- salt and pepper to taste

Method:

1. Prepare a medium frying pan, add oil and sauté the onions and garlic, cook until soft, approx. 5 minutes.
2. Add the beef and cook for another ten minutes.
3. Next, add the zucchini, chicken broth, thyme, oregano, parsley, also a dash of salt and pepper. Cover and simmer for thirty minutes or until zucchini is smooth.
4. When done, use a spoon and take the mixture and put it into a mixing bowl to allow it to cool.
5. Whisk eggs in another bowl and put into meat blend, add feta, and blend well.
6. Pour into an oven safe bowl.
7. Add more feta if you like (optional).
8. Put in a preheated oven at 350F for about 25-30 minutes, or until eggs are cooked and dish is set.

Greek Breakfast Wrap

Serves: 3-4

Ingredients:

- 6-7 medium-large egg whites
- 14 oz turkey sausage
- 2-3 multigrain tortillas (your choice, depending on size of each warp)
- 2 peppers (diced and seeds removed)
- ½ cup kalamata olives (chopped)
- ½ cup crumbled feta

Method:

1. Dice up olives and peppers.
2. Within an oiled skillet over low-medium heat, add olives and peppers and sauté for a few moments.
3. Next, add the turkey sausage and cook for about 5 minutes or until done.
4. While carrying this out, add egg whites to a medium bowl and whisk.
5. When the turkey sausage is cooked, add egg whites and mix occasionally.
6. Cook until eggs are done, about 2-4 minutes.
7. Reduce from stove and place about half of the mixture on a warm tortilla. Add a dash of feta, roll and wrap, cut in two and placed on plate.
8. Ready to serve.

Greek Yogurt Pancakes

Serves: 3-5

Ingredients:

- 1 medium-large egg
- 1 shot glass
- ½ cup cottage cheese
- ½ teaspoon vanilla extract
- ½ teaspoon lemon extract
- ½ cup Greek Yogurt
- ½ teaspoon baking soda
- ½ cup fruit of your choice
- ⅔ cup all-purpose flour
- ¼ cup sugar
- ¼ teaspoon salt

Method:

1. Inside a bowl, mix flour, sugar, baking soda, and salt.
2. Next, add the Greek yogurt, egg, cottage cheese, vanilla, and lemon. Blend until a batter is created.
3. Heat skillet on med-high heat.
4. Utilizing a shot glass (or your choice), fill up with the batter and put on hot skillet.
5. Cook until bubbles start to form at the top and sides become somewhat solid, approx. 3-4 min.
6. Turnover and cook for another 2-3 min, or until it turns golden brown.
7. Repeat the process with the rest of the batter.
8. Serve warm with your selection of sliced fruits and syrup/butter.

Greek Breakfast Omelet

Serves: 2

Ingredients:

- 6 medium-large eggs (whisked)
- 2 cloves garlic (minced)
- 2 tablespoons crumbled feta cheese
- 1 tablespoon butter
- 1 tablespoon extra-virgin olive oil
- 1 cup spinach
- 1/2 teaspoon dried basil
- 1/2 teaspoon dried oregano
- 1/4 cup milk
- 1/4 cup kalamata olives, sliced
- 1/4 cup roasted red peppers (chopped)
- 1/4 cup marinated artichoke hearts (chopped)
- 1/4 teaspoon salt
- 1/4 teaspoon pepper
- 1/4 cup cherry tomatoes (halved)

Method:

1. Inside a bowl, whisk moderately the eggs and milk. Set it aside.
2. Heat 1 tablespoon of butter and olive oil in a big skillet, set to medium heat. Add spinach and garlic and sauté for approximately 30 seconds, or until spinach is soft. Add roasted red peppers, seasoning and artichokes. Sautee for 1-2 minutes, or until vegetables soften. Remove from skillet and set it aside.
3. Pour the egg and milk mix into skillet and allow it sit for approximately 30 secs. Add the spinach blend, tomatoes, olives, feta cheese onto fifty percent of the omelet. Add more seasoning if desired. Cook for about

3-4 minutes, or until eggs completely done. Fold omelet in two and scoop onto a plate.
4. Add feta toppings and cheese if desired.

Moustokouloura (Grape must cook)

Serves: 10-15

Ingredients:

- 1 1/2 kg flour
- 4 teaspoon baking powder
- 1 cup olive oil (or oil of your choice)
- 1 cup sugar
- 1 cup grape must
- 1 cup orange juice
- 1 teaspoon baking soda
- 1 teaspoon cinnamon
- 1 teaspoon clove
- 1/2 cup brandy

Method:

1. Use a mixing bowl and mix the oil, the grape must and the sugar until it blends evenly.
2. Dissolved the baking soda and add the brandy, the cinnamon, the clove and the orange juice.
3. Steadily add the flour and the cooking powder and combine. Use the dough to create the cookies in the form that you want.
4. Bake in a preheated oven at 180° for 15-20 minutes depending on the size of the cookies.

Kalitsounia - Cretan Sweet Cheese Pastries

Serves: 6-8

Ingredients:

For the dough:

- 1kg flour (35 ounces)
- 4 teaspoons baking powder
- 1 1/2 cup of sugar
- 1 medium-large egg
- 1 cup olive oil
- 1 cup strained yogurt
- juice of 1/2 orange
- zest of 1 lemon (optional)
- 1/2 teaspoon vanilla extract (optional)

For the filling:

- 1kg (35 ounces) of fresh soft myzithra cheese or mascarpone or ricotta
- 1 cup of sugar
- 1 medium egg and 1 egg white
- 1 teaspoon powdered cinnamon

For the topping:

- 2 medium eggs
- 1 tablespoon water
- 1 tablespoon powdered cinnamon

Method:

1. To prepare the dough for the cheese pastries (kalitsounia), add into a big bowl the olive oil, sugar, eggs

and yogurt; blend well using your hands, until it's mix properly. Pour in the orange juice, the lemon zest and vanilla extract and mix again. Sieve the flour with the baking powder and add steadily to the mixture. Knead the dough with your hands, until it softens. With regards to the flour, you may want to use a bit less or even more flour than the recipe demands. The dough should be smooth, however, not sticky.

2. Leave the dough to rest for approximately 30 minutes.
3. In the meantime, prepare the filling for the kalitsounia. Mash the cheese into a big bowl, add the sugar, the eggs and the cinnamon; mix thoroughly.
4. Place the dough on the floured surface; utilizing a rolling pin, stretch the dough to a width around 0.3 cm. Using a 10cm cutter, slice out some circles. (If you discover it difficult to roll the complete dough, divide it in two and roll each separately).
5. Put in a spoonful of the cheese mix in the center of each dough and spread. Raise the rim of the dough up round the cheese and making use of your fingertips, pinch the sides to draw the dough in across the cheese, leaving the center open.
6. Preheat the oven to 180-200C. Place the cheese pastries (kalitsounia) on a sizable baking holder, lined with parchment paper and leave to rest for 20 minutes. Into a bowl, whisk 1-2 eggs and 1 tablespoon of water and brush the pastries. Sprinkle with cinnamon powder and bake for approximately 25 minutes, until it turns golden.

Boureki

Serves: 8

Ingredients:

- 3 lbs. medium-large zucchini (washed and sliced into thin rounds)
- 2 lbs. medium-large potatoes (peeled and cut into thin rounds)
- 1 lb. ricotta cheese or anthotiro (crumbled)
- 1/2 lb. mizithra or parmesan cheese (grated)
- 4 -5 garlic cloves (minced)
- 1 large onion (chopped)
- 2 tablespoons of fresh mint (minced, 1 tablespoon dried)
- 3/4 cup olive oil
- 1/2 cup flour
- 1/4 cup water
- salt and pepper to taste

Method:

1. Preheat your oven to 350F (170C).
2. Place the zucchini, potato and onion into a deep bowl, add 1/2 glass flour and add a dash of salt and pepper to flavor (careful! the cheese will have plenty of salt, avoid too much), all the grated cheese, mint, garlic, olive oil, and toss to coat all slices.
3. Pour this mixture into a greased (olive oil) 13 X 9" pyrex cooking dish (this doesn't need to be pretty, it will not show much when cooked and sliced up. Flavor is everything!).
4. Press down with hands to relatively small size. Carefully put 1/4 glass water over top.

5. Bake for approximately one hour and 20 minutes. (if boureki is apparently too dried out during baking, you can include up to 1/4 glass more water - but careful, the zucchini and potatoes will also release water during cooking).
6. Allow to cool for about 15 minutes before you cut into it.

Froutalia Omelet

Serves: 4-6

Ingredients:

- 1 kg medium potatoes
- 4-5 medium-large eggs
- 4 spoonful of pork fat
- 2-3 traditional Greek sausages
- 2 spoonful of minced cheese (local if possible or else hard, yellow cheese)
- some milk
- some peppermint or marjoram
- salt and pepper to taste

Method:

1. Peel and cut the potatoes in round shape.
2. Put the pork fat in a pan and then the sausages and once it is melted, add the potatoes all together.
3. Stir the potatoes until they get soft and roasted brown.
4. In a bowl, scramble the eggs and add the milk, the salt, pepper and the minced cheese, the peppermint or the marjoram. Pour the mixture in the pan and leave it until it is well baked from the one side.
5. Then use a large plate or cover in the size of the pan and turn over the fourtalia, so as to be baked from the other side as well.
6. Fourtalia is served in a round platter.

Bougatsa

Serves: 3-4

Ingredients:

For the bougatsa:

- 1kg (35 ounces) milk
- 400-450g (15 ounces) phyllo dough
- 200g (7 ounces) butter, melted
- 200g (7 ounces) sugar
- 120g (4.5 ounces) all-purpose flour
- 4 medium eggs
- 1 teaspoon vanilla extract

For the topping:

- ground cinnamon
- icing sugar

Method:

1. To create this traditional bougatsa formula, begin by making the filling (steps 1-3). To prepare the filling for the bougatsa, prepare a large bowl and add the sugar, flour and eggs; whisk thoroughly.
2. Pour into a saucepan the milk and the vanilla extract and bring to a boil. Before the milk comes to a boil, ladle 1/3 of the milk in to the flour mix and stir.
3. Turn heat down and add the flour mixture in to the saucepan with the rest of the warm milk. Whisk rapidly, until mix has thickened and it is easy and creamy. (Do not remove the skillet from the stove.) This will take about 2-3 minutes. Remove the skillet from the stove and stir occasionally, to keep the custard from forming a skin

on top, when you prepare all of those other bougatsa formula.

4. For this bougatsa recipe you will need a big baking tray, approx. 20×30 cm. Utilizing a pastry brush, butter the bottom and sides.

5. Unroll the phyllo dough from the plastic sleeve. To create this bougatsa formula you'll need 10-12 phyllo linens. Use 5-6 bedding of phyllo for bottom of the bougatsa and 4-5 bed linens for the very best.

6. Start by layering the sheets one at a time on the bottom of the tray, ensuring to sprinkle each one completely with melted butter. Tip in the custard, smoothing the top with a spatula and fold the phyllo sheet flaps on the custard. Top the bougatsa with 4-5 phyllo linens, sprinkling each sheet with melted butter. Having a blade trim a few of the excessive phyllo, if you want, and roll the others on the sides. Brush the top with enough butter and slit the top of the bougatsa with a knife.

7. Bake the bougatsa in preheated oven at 160 for 45 minutes, until phyllo is crisp and turns color to golden brown.

8. Allow bougatsa cool off for some time before serving and sprinkle with icing sugars and cinnamon.

9. Enjoy while still warm with tea or coffee.

Chapter Two: Greek Lunch Recipes

Pastitsio

Serves: 24

Ingredients:

For the main dish:

- 1 pkg. (500g) macaroni for Pastitsio - available at Greek or ethnic groceries. Or you can substitute it with ziti or penne
- 2 lbs. ground beef (or ground lamb, or a mixture of both)
- 1 14 oz. can tomato puree or sauce
- 4 medium egg whites (reserve the yolks for bechamel sauce)
- 3 tablespoons breadcrumbs
- 3 tablespoons chopped fresh parsley
- 1 1/2 cups grated Parmesan cheese (or Kefalotyri if available)
- 1 large yellow onion (chopped)
- 1 teaspoon ground cinnamon
- 1 cup dry white wine
- 1/2 cup olive oil
- 1/2 teaspoon ground allspice
- 1/2 cup (1 stick) unsalted butter
- salt and pepper to taste

For the bechamel sauce:

- 8 medium egg yolks (beaten lightly)
- 1 cup (2 sticks) unsalted butter
- 1 cup all-purpose flour

- 1-quart milk, warmed
- a dash of ground nutmeg

Method:

Begin with the meat filling:

1. Heat olive oil in a large sauté pan. Add ground beef and cook over medium-high heat until somewhat cooked, approx. 5 minutes. Add onions and cook until they are soft, approx. 5 minutes more.
2. Add wine, tomato sauce, parsley, allspice, cinnamon, salt, and pepper and allow sauce to simmer over low heat for about 10 minutes.
3. While the sauce is simmering, put water on to boil the pasta.
4. Cook the pasta drain well. Rinse the pasta in colander under cold water to cool them slightly.
5. Stir in 3 tablespoons of breadcrumbs to meat sauce to absorb excess liquid. Remove from heat.
6. Melt 1/2 cup butter in pasta pot and return cooked pasta to the pot. Stir in beaten egg whites and 1 cup of grated cheese and toss slowly, being careful not to break the pasta.
7. Brush the bottom and sides of the pan with olive oil. Layer the bottom with half the pasta noodles and press down so that they are somewhat flat.
8. Add the meat filling in an even layer to the pasta. Top with remaining pasta noodles and flatten top layer evenly.
9. Pre-heat the oven to 350 degrees while you prepare the bechamel sauce.

Bechamel sauce:

1. Melt butter in a saucepan over low heat. Using a whisk, add flour to melted butter whisking continuously to

make a smooth paste or roux. Allow the flour/butter mixture to cook for a minute but do not allow it to brown.

2. Add warmed milk to mixture in a steady stream, whisking continuously. Simmer over low heat until it thickens but does not boil.

3. Remove from heat and stir in beaten egg yolks. Add pinch of nutmeg. If sauce still needs to thicken, return to heat and cook over very low heat while continuing to stir.

4. Bechamel is thicker than gravy but not quite as thick as pudding. It should be somewhere in between. One way to tell if it is thick enough is to dip your wooden spoon in the sauce and draw your finger across the back of the spoon.

5. If the sauce holds a visible line then it is thick enough.

6. Pour the bechamel over the pasta noodles making sure to pour sauce down in to the corners as well. Sprinkle with remaining 1/2 cup of grated Parmesan cheese. Bake in 350-degree oven for approximately 45 minutes or until the top is a nice golden color.

Horiatiki Salata (Greek Salad)

Serves: 1

Ingredients:

- 4-5 medium-large ripe tomatoes
- 1 dozen Greek olives (Kalamata, green Cretan olives, etc.)
- 1 cucumber
- 1 green bell pepper
- 1 large red onion
- 1 tablespoon of water
- 1/4-pound Greek feta cheese, (sliced or crumbled)
- garnish: pickled pepperoncini hot peppers (garnish)
- garnish: salt to taste, dried oregano (garnish)
- garnish: dried oregano (garnish)
- top quality extra virgin olive oil to taste (garnish)
- pepper (optional)

Method:

1. Clean and dried out the tomatoes, cucumber and green pepper. Clean the outer from the onion, wash and dry.
2. Slice the tomatoes into bite-sized chunks, removing the core. Salt lightly. Cut the cucumber into 1/4-in. slices, cutting pieces in two (you can peel off the cucumber if you like). Lightly salt. Cut the pepper into bands, eliminating the stem and seeds. Salt lightly. Cut the onion into thin rings.
3. Mix the tomatoes, cucumbers, green pepper and onion in a big salad bowl. Sprinkle with oregano, put olive oil on the salad, and toss.
4. Before serving, place the feta together with the salad, either as slices or crumbled, and sprinkle the cheese with oregano (and pepper, if desired). Toss in a few olives.

25

5. Add a small amount of olive oil with water and drizzle.
6. Serve garnished with hot peppers.

Saganaki (Pan-seared Greek Cheese)

Serves: 1

Ingredients:

- 1-pound firm cheese (graviera cheese if available)
- 2 to 3 lemons (quartered)
- 2/3 cup all-purpose flour for dredging
- 1 tablespoon olive oil

Method:

1. Slice the cheese into pieces or wedges 1/2-in. solid by 2 1/2 to 3 ins wide. Each cut must be solid enough that it generally does not melt during cooking.
2. Moisten each cut with cool water and dredge it in the flour. Get rid of any extra flour.
3. Heat about 1 tablespoon of the oil over medium-high heat in a sagani or small heavy-bottomed frying skillet. Cast iron is most effective.
4. Sear each cheese cut in the warmed oil until it's turns brown, flipping the cut midway to brownish both sides equally.
5. Serve hot with a press of lemon juice.

Variation and tips:

- The main element for success with this dish is to get the oil as hot as you possibly can before cooking the cheese, but don't allow it begin to smoke.
- Use a firm cheese that will endure against heat. Authentic Greek cooking usually uses graviera, kefalotyri, or kefalograviera. Halloumi is used in Cyprus traditionally, while chefs on the island of Chios choose mastello. You can even use pecorino romano if you are in a pinch.

- For variation, you can drop the floured cheese into a beaten egg before frying.
- In the event that you like a little pepper, then add newly ground dark pepper to the flour before dredging the cheese.
- For any flaming version of saganaki, move the finished cheese to a clean skillet or sagani. Pour a dash of ouzo over it and light it with a match, then douse the flames with the lemon juice. This is not a Greek custom, but it's rather a showstopper at gatherings and celebrations.

Fassolakia Lathera (Greek Green Bean Casserole)

Serves: 3-4

Ingredients:

- 4-5 ripe medium tomatoes (skinned and crushed, or you can replace it with 1 cup canned crushed tomatoes)
- 2-3 medium-large potatoes (cut in large wedges)
- A large handful of baby carrots
- 2 lbs. green beans (cleaned and trimmed)
- 2 tablespoons tomato paste
- 2 cloves garlic (minced)
- 1½ cups warm water
- 1 teaspoon sugar
- 1 large onion (diced)
- 1 tablespoon chopped fresh dill
- 1/2 cup olive oil
- 1/2 cup chopped fresh parsley
- Salt and pepper to taste

Method:

1. In a big Dutch oven or pot, heat the olive oil over medium-high temperature. Add the onion and sauté until soft. Add the garlic and sauté until fragrant, about a minute.
2. Add the green beans, potatoes, and carrots to the container. Dissolve the tomato paste in water and add, combined with the smashed tomatoes, parsley, and sugar. Lower heat to low and simmer with the cover for about one hour or before green beans are tender, but not mushy.
3. Within the last 10 minutes of cooking, add the chopped fresh dill and season with salt and pepper to taste.

Fassolatha (White Bean Soup)

Serves: 3-4

Ingredients:

- 1 lb. dried white beans (your choice)
- 1 - 14 oz. can diced plum tomatoes (un-drained)
- 10 cups water
- 2 medium carrots (diced)
- 2 ribs celery (diced)
- 2 tablespoons tomato paste
- 1 medium-large onion (diced)
- 1 bay leaf
- 1/2 cup olive oil
- 1/4 cup fresh parsley (chopped, for garnish)
- salt and pepper to taste

Method:

Quick soaking method:

1. Add beans plus enough water to drown the beans by 2 inches to a pot. Add 2 tablespoons of salt and stir. Bring beans to a boil. Switch off heat, cover, and soak for one hour. Drain and wash beans under cool water before using.

For the soup:

1. Add the beans, water, and olive oil to a big, non-reactive soup container and bring to a boil. Reduce heat and simmer until beans are soft however, not mushy, approx. one hour.
2. Add vegetables, tomatoes, tomato paste, and bay leaf to the container and simmer uncovered for another 30-45

minutes so that the flavors blend well and the soup thicken a little.

3. Season the soup with salt and pepper to taste. Take away the bay leaf and sprinkle with cut fresh parsley before serving.

Note:

- Adding an acidic component like tomato to the soup prior to the beans are prepared can toughen the skins on the coffee beans.

Fakes Soupa – Lentil Soup

Serves: 1-2

Ingredients:

- 1-pound ripe tomatoes (puréed)
- 4 1/4 cups water
- 2 bay leaves
- 2 cloves garlic (finely chopped)
- 1 small red onion (finely chopped)
- 1 cup olive oil
- 1/2-pound small lentils (rinsed)
- 1/4 cup red wine vinegar, or to taste
- dash of sea salt
- dash of freshly ground pepper

Method:

1. Add water, tomatoes, bay leaves, onion, and garlic to a heavy-bottomed container.

2. Bring to a slow boil over medium heat, then add the lentils and olive oil.
3. Reduce heat and simmer partly covered for approximately 1 to 1 1/2 hours or before lentils are soft.
4. Remove from heat and remove the bay leaves. Season with salt and pepper.
5. Mix in the vinegar or serve on the side, and perhaps a part of crusty breads.

Variation and tips:

- The total cooking time will depend on the type of lentils you use.
- Increase the water to 5 1/2 cups if you want to prepare this soup without tomatoes.
- You can add a pinch of Greek oregano or rosemary to the soup along with the bay leaves, but if you're making it without tomatoes then leave these out.
- If you're pressed for time and don't feel comfortable letting the soup simmer for an hour or more while you're occupied, you can soak the lentils in water for up to two hours before cooking. You can cut the simmering time down to about 20 to 35 minutes, but cover the pot if you shorten the time.
- As with any soup, cooks are known for adding their own personal touches to *fakes soupa*. Some add diced potatoes or carrots.
- The Greeks like to top this dish with crumbled feta cheese.

Arni me Patates (Roast Leg of Lamb With Oven Roasted Potatoes)

Serves: 5-6

Ingredients:

- 1 leg of lamb (bone in, trimmed of excess fat)
- 5 lbs. medium-large potatoes (peeled and cut into wedges)

For the marinade:

- 4 cloves garlic (chopped)
- 2 lemons (juiced)
- 2 sprigs of rosemary (leaves stripped from stem)
- 2 tablespoons coarse salt
- 1 teaspoon black pepper freshly ground
- 3/4 cup olive oil

For the potatoes:

- 2 lemons (juiced)
- 2 teaspoons dried oregano
- 1 teaspoon garlic powder
- 1 teaspoon dried rosemary
- 1/4 cup olive oil (for drizzling)
- dash salt
- dash black pepper (freshly ground)

Method:

1. Preheat your oven to 425 degrees.
2. Add the potatoes to a big bowl. Drizzle with olive oil and then season with some salt and pepper. Add the garlic powder, oregano, and rosemary and toss the potatoes well to cover.

3. Place the potatoes in the bottom of the roasting pan and empty some space in the center. Lay the leg of lamb on top of the potatoes.
4. Roast at 425 degrees for about 20 minutes. Lower the temperature the 350 degrees and continue to roast without cover. A 9-pound leg will take approximately 3 hours to cook.
5. Make sure to baste the potatoes and the lamb with pan juices while they are cooking.
6. It's best to use a meat thermometer to check doneness because ovens tend to vary. I like to remove the lamb from the oven when a thermometer inserted into the meatiest part of the leg reaches 155 degrees (F).
7. Remove the leg of lamb to a platter, put a cover, and allow it to rest for at least 15 minutes before slicing.
8. While the lamb is resting, you can increase the heat of the oven to a low broil setting and give the potatoes a little extra color if required. Otherwise, remove the potatoes to a platter, give them a squeeze of lemon and a sprinkle of salt and then serve with the sliced lamb.

For the marinade:

1. Add the ingredients to a blender or food processor and process until soft. The consistency of the marinade should be thicker so it doesn't run off the meat while cooking and forms a crust.
2. Put the meat in a big roasting pan. Brush the marinade on in thick layer covering as much meat as possible. Refrigerate until ready to roast.

Classic Greek Eggplant Moussaka

Serves: 3-4

Ingredients:

*For   the
vegetables:*

- 8 medium-large egg whites (keep the yolks for the béchamel)
- 3-4 eggplants
- 2 cups plain breadcrumbs
- 1-pound medium potatoes
- olive oil (for greasing baking sheets)
- salt to taste

For the meat filling:

- 1 1/2 pounds ground beef or lamb
- 2 tablespoons tomato paste
- 2 cloves garlic (minced)
- 2 large onions (diced)
- 1 teaspoon ground cinnamon
- 1 cup crushed tomatoes
- 1 teaspoon sugar
- 1/2 cup dry red wine
- 1/4 teaspoon ground allspice
- 1/4 cup fresh parsley (chopped)
- salt and pepper to taste

For the bechamel sauce:

- 8 medium-large egg yolks (slightly beaten)
- 4 cups warm milk
- 1 cup (2 sticks) unsalted butter

- 1 cup all-purpose flour
- dash of ground nutmeg

For the assembly:

- breadcrumbs (for the bottom of the pan)
- 1 cup grated Kefalotyri or Parmesan cheese

Method:

Prepare the vegetables:

1. Use a sharp peeler to partially peel the eggplants, leaving strips of peel about 1-inch wide around the eggplant. Slice the eggplant into 1/2-inch slices.
2. Put the eggplant slices in a colander and salt them generously. Cover them with an inverted plate and weigh down the plate with a heavy can or jar. Place the colander in the sink and let it sit for about 15 to 20 minutes, preferably 1 hour.
3. Remove the potatoes skin, place whole in a pot, drown with cold water, and bring to a boil. Cook until they are just about done, approx. 10 minutes. They shouldn't get too soft, just cook it enough so that they no longer crunch. Drain, cool, and cut them into 1/4-inch slices. Set aside.
4. Heat the oven to 400F. Line two baking sheets with aluminum foil and slightly grease with oil.
5. Add a splash of water to the egg whites and beat them lightly. Place breadcrumbs on a flat plate.
6. Rinse the eggplant slices and dry with paper towels to remove excess water. Dip the eggplant slices in the beaten egg whites and then dredge them in the breadcrumbs, coating both sides.
7. Put breaded eggplant slices on the foil-lined baking sheets and bake for about 30 minutes, turning them over once during cooking.

8. When eggplant is finished cooking, set aside and lower the oven temperature to 350F.

Meat filling:

1. In a large pan, cook the beef until the pink color disappears. Add onion and sauté until soft, approx. 5 minutes. Add garlic and cook until fragrant, approx. 1 minute.
2. Pour wine to the pan and allow it to simmer and reduce a bit before adding cinnamon, allspice, parsley, tomato paste, crushed tomatoes, and sugar.
3. Let the sauce simmer, without cover, for about 15 minutes so that excess liquid can evaporate. The sauce should be be drier and chunkier. Season to taste with salt and pepper.

Bechamel sauce:

1. Melt butter in a big saucepan over low-medium heat. Add flour to melted butter, whisking constantly to make a smooth paste. Let the flour cook for a minute but don't allow it to brown.
2. Pour warmed milk to the mixture in a steady stream, whisking constantly. Simmer over low heat until it thickens a bit but doesn't boil.
3. Put away from heat, and stir in beaten egg yolks and a dash of nutmeg. Return to the heat and stir until sauce thickens. Set aside.

Assemble the Moussaka:

1. Slightly grease a big deep baking pan (you can use a lasagna pan). Sprinkle the bottom of the pan with breadcrumbs.
2. Leaving a 1/4-inch space around the edges of the pan, put the potatoes in a layer on the bottom. Top with a layer of half of the eggplant slices.

3. Add the meat sauce on top of the eggplant layer and sprinkle with 1/4 of the grated cheese. Put another layer of eggplant slices on top of it and sprinkle again with 1/4 of the grated cheese.
4. Pour the béchamel sauce over all, make sure to allow the sauce to fill the sides and corners of the pan. Smooth the béchamel on top with a spatula and sprinkle with remaining grated cheese.
5. Bake for about 45 minutes or until béchamel sauce is a nice golden-brown color. Allow it to cool for about 15 to 20 minutes before slicing and serving.

Grilled Pork Souvlaki

Serves: 3-4

Ingredients:

For the marinade:

- 4 cloves garlic (chopped and finely minced)
- 2 tablespoons freshly squeezed lemon juice
- 1 tablespoon dried mint
- 1 tablespoon dried oregano
- 1 bay leaf (crumbled into small pieces)
- 1/4 cup olive oil
- 1/4 cup red wine

For the kabobs:

- 1 lb. pork shoulder (trimmed of fat and cut into 1 1/4-inch cubes)
- 2-3 wedges of lemon (for serving)
- salt and pepper to taste

Method:

1. In a big non-reactive bowl, whisk together all the marinade ingredients. Add the pork cubes, put a plastic wrap cover refrigerate for about 2 to 3 hours.
2. If you're using wooden skewers, soak these in a shallow pan filled with water while the meat marinates.
3. Set the temperature of the grill to medium-high. Thread the meat onto the skewers (about 6-7 pieces per skewer). Season the pork with salt and black pepper.
4. Grill over medium-high heat for about 10 minutes, turning occasionally until they are cooked through.
5. Squeeze some fresh lemon juice over the meat before serving.

Bakaliaros Tiganitos (Fried Salt Cods)

Serves: 4

Ingredients:

- 1 – 1 1/2 lbs. salt cod
- 2 cups self-rising flour
- 2 cups water
- canola or vegetable oil for frying
- salt and pepper to taste

Method:

Preparing the fish:

1. Wash the fish under cold water and remove any scales or visible bones. Soak in cold water for at least 12 hours, changing out the water a few times. Cut the fish into 2-inch pieces and set aside on a plate.

Making the batter:

1. Put the flour into a large bowl. Using a whisk, slowly whisk in the water until a thick batter form. it should be thick so that it can adhere to the fish without running off. Season the batter generously with salt and pepper.
2. In a large skillet pan, heat the oil over to medium-high heat until a droplet of water sizzles and jumps when dropped in the pan. If you have an oil/candy thermometer, the temperature of the oil should be at least 350 F (175 C).
3. Dip the fish in the batter and slowly place it in the hot oil. Fry the fish until golden brown on each side then remove and drain on paper towels to remove excess oil. Place the fish on a baking rack over a sheet pan in a warm oven to keep it warm and crisp until ready to serve.
4. Serve with the delicious garlic dip known as Skordalia and enjoy.

Homemade Gyro

Serves: 4

Ingredients:

Meat mixture:

- 1 lbs. ground lamb or beef
- 2 cloves garlic (chopped)
- 2 teaspoon salt
- 2 teaspoon fresh lemon juice
- 1 1/2 teaspoon cumin
- 1 teaspoon black pepper
- 1 teaspoon dried oregano
- 1/4 cup red onion (chopped)
- 1/4 teaspoon nutmeg

For the sandwich:

- 4 rounds flatbread or pita
- 1 tomato (sliced)
- 1 onion (sliced)
- 1 leaf of lettuce
- Tzatziki sauce

Method:

To make the meat mixture:

1. The first step in making any gyro is to prepare the meat. It's very easy and should take just a few minutes, but you will need to let it marinade for about an hour, so plan in advance.
2. Combine all the ingredients thoroughly in a medium bowl.

3. Divide into four equal portions and shape into oblong patties about 3" wide, 6" long, 1/2" thick.
4. Notice that the patty is shaped more like a sausage - long and thin - rather than a hamburger patty. This is intentional, to ensure the patty fits in the flatbread.
5. Refrigerate for one hour.

To build the sandwich:

1. You can grill the patties on your outdoor grill or fry them up in a pan on the stove. The main thing is to have edges on the patty crisp.
2. The toppings that go into a traditional gyro are simple: tzatziki, lettuce, tomato, and onion. You can skip the onion if you prefer because there are already onions in the meat.
3. Grill the patties over medium-high heat for about 3 to 4 minutes per side.
4. Spread tzatziki sauce down the center of a flatbread round.
5. Add a lettuce leaf, some diced tomato, and a few thin onion slices.
6. Add the patty, fold the bread over the lamb, and enjoy.

Tip:

▪ Gyros are a bit messy to eat. You can wrap each gyro in foil to avoid it falling apart.

Dolmathakia Me Kima (Stuffed Grape Leaves With Meat and Rice)

Serves: 2

Ingredients:

- 1 (16-ounce) grape leaves in brine (about 70 leaves)
- 8 cups water
- 1/2 lemon juice only
- 1 teaspoon sea salt
- grape leaves

Filling:

- 2 pounds lean ground beef (or lamb, or a mix of both)
- 5 tablespoons olive oil (divided)
- 2 1/2 lemons (juiced and cut in half)
- 2 cups of water
- 2 medium-large onions (finely chopped)
- 1 bunch fresh dill (chopped)
- 1 tablespoon mint leaves (chopped)
- 1 cup short-grain rice (uncooked)
- 1/4 teaspoon pepper

Method:

1. Bring 8 cups of water to a boil in a big container, and add the juice of 1/2 lemon and the salt. Carefully unroll the leaves (do not separate them). Switch off heat and place the leaves in the warm water for about three minutes.
2. Take away the leaves and place them in a dish and cover with cool water. When it's cooled, drain in a colander. It isn't unusual for most of the external leaves in the jar to

43

be broken or rip while using. Arranged these apart to use later in the mixture.

3. To get the filling ready, begin by soaking the rice for ten minutes in warm water and drain. (Alternatively, sauté the rice with the onion.)

4. Sauté the onions in 1 tablespoon of olive oil until soft, but not browned.

5. Combine the onion, floor beef, rice, olive oil, dill, mint, juice of just one 1 lemon, and pepper in a medium bowl. Blend well using your hand.

6. To fill up and roll the leaves, softly separate and place it shiny-side down on a work surface. Place a pinch (up to teaspoon) of the filling up on the leaf at the stage where the stem joins the leaf.

7. Fold up the bottom of the leaf on the filling, then each part inward in parallel folds, and roll-up the leaf. The roll should be firm, not tight, as the filling up will increase during cooking. Do it again until all the filling has been used.

8. Because the leaves on the bottom can burn while the filling cooks, put a plate or wooden souvlaki skewers in the bottom of a heavy-bottomed pot. The plate should fit comfortly in the pot.

9. If there are unused leaves or leaves that were torn and not used during the filling process, put them on the plate or on top of the skewers. Place the dolmathakia on top, packing them closely together (not squashed), seam side down, so they don't unroll during cooking. Layer them until all are in the pot (two to three layers are best, but no more than four layers). Place several unused leaves over the top.

10. Take another plate and place it upside down on top of the dolmathakia, using something to weigh it down (a second plate works well). Add the 2 cups of water to the pot and cover. Bring the water to a gentle boil, add the remaining juice from the 1 1/2 lemons, reduce heat to low

and simmer for approximately 50 to 70 minutes. Check to see if done—if the rice has cooked, they are done. If not, continue cooking for another 10 minutes and check again. Cooking time depends both on the type of pot used and the particular stovetop heating element.

11. If preferred, you can use a pressure cooker. No plates are needed but do use the skewers in the bottom. Pack the dolmathakia into the pressure cooker, add the 2 cups of water, close and cook for 15 to 20 minutes at the first pressure mark.

Yemista Me Ryzi (Greek Stuffed Vegetables with Rice Recipe)

Serves: 2

Ingredients:

- 4 firm medium tomatoes
- 4 medium-large zucchinis
- 4 small eggplants
- 4 peppers (green bell, Cubanelle, or Anaheim)
- 2 medium carrots (grated)
- 1 1/2 cups of long grain rice
- 1 spring onion (chopped)
- 1 bunch of fresh parsley (chopped)
- 1 pound of zucchini (grated)
- 1 cup of olive oil (divided)
- 1 tablespoon of sea salt
- 1 teaspoon of freshly ground pepper
- 1/2 eggplant (peeled and grated)
- toasted breadcrumbs (garnish)

Method:

1. Wash and dry the vegetables. Cut the caps off the tomatoes, peppers, and eggplant, and both ends off the zucchini and set aside.
2. Scoop out the pulp and seeds from the eggplant, zucchini, and peppers with a spoon and discard.
3. Scoop out the tomato pulp, chop well, and set aside. Slightly salt the inside of all vegetables.
4. Heat 1/2 cup of olive oil in a pot, and sauté the onion for about 2-3 minutes.
5. Add the grated zucchini, eggplant, and carrots, and cook over low heat for about 10 minutes.

46

6. Add the tomato pulp and continue to cook for another 5 minutes.
7. Remove from the heat and set aside to cool for about 15 minutes, then transfer to a bowl.
8. Add the rice, salt, and pepper, and mix thoroughly.
9. Using a spoon, fill vegetables loosely with the rice mixture, place in a roasting pan packed closely but not squashed, with caps covering the tops and ends.
10. Place tomatoes (and small bell peppers if used) upright, lie the others on their sides.
11. Pour 1/2 cup olive oil and 1/2 cup water over the top, sprinkle the tops of the upright vegetables with toasted breadcrumbs, and bake at 450F (230C) for 1 hour.
12. Halfway through, turn the vegetables that are placed on their sides.
13. Note: If the vegetables start to get too brown before cooking time is up, cover with foil.

Tip:

- Scoop out vegetables leaving a thin shell, about 1/4 inch.

Htapothi Sti Skhara (Greek Grilled Octopus)

Serves: 3-4

Ingredients:

- 4 1/2 pounds fresh octopus, (or frozen and defrosted)
- 1/2 cup olive oil (to coat)
- 1/2 cup extra-virgin olive oil
- 1/2 tablespoon crushed Greek oregano
- 1/4 cup freshly squeezed lemon juice

Method:

1. Put water in a large pot and bring it to a boil. Place the whole octopus in the pot making sure there is enough boiling water to cover generously. When it resumes boiling, cook for 10 minutes. Remove from the heat and drain.
2. When it's cool enough to handle, rub the octopus with your hands under running water to remove the dark outer membrane. This comes off quite easy. It's alright if it doesn't all come off.
3. Put the octopus in the pressure cooker with enough water to cover. Bring to a boil, seal, and when pressure is reached, lower the heat and cook for 10 minutes. Use quick pressure release, remove the octopus, and drain.
4. Preheat the grill. When the octopus is cool enough to handle, cut off the tentacles, and cut the head sac into 1/2-inch strips.
5. Brush with olive oil (or brush the grill) and grill over low coals for about 45 minutes to 1 hour (test for tenderness). Just before serving, cut tentacles into 3/4- to 1-inch pieces on a diagonal.
6. Make the sauce by mixing the extra-virgin olive oil and lemon juice in the blender until it thickens (this should

take just a few seconds). Pour over the octopus, sprinkle with oregano, and serve. For a different taste, serve grilled octopus with slices of lime.

Keftethes (Greek Beef Meatballs)

Serves: 3-4

Ingredients:

- 2 pounds ground beef
- 2 tablespoons grated cheese
- 2 onions (finely chopped or grated)
- 2 cloves garlic (finely minced)
- 1 medium egg (slightly beaten)
- 1 tablespoon dried mint
- 1 cup breadcrumbs
- 1/2 cup milk
- 1/4 cup chopped fresh parsley
- olive oil (for greasing baking sheet)
- salt and freshly ground black pepper (garnish)

Method:

1. Preheat your oven to 375F. Line a baking sheet with aluminum foil and lightly grease with either olive oil or cooking spray.
2. In a big bowl, mix all the ingredients and blend well. Cover with plastic wrap and allow mixture to sit in the refrigerator for at least 1 hour.
3. Make the meat mixture into balls about the size of a walnut. Place on the greased baking sheet about 1 inch apart.
4. Bake for about 40 minutes, turning the meatballs midway through the cooking time.
5. Allow the meatballs to cool before serving.

Keftedes Arni (Lamb Meatballs)

Serves: 3-4

Ingredients:

- 1 kg (35 oz.) lamb
- 1 large red onion (grated)
- 2 cloves of garlic (minced)
- 2 tablespoons fresh mint (chopped)
- 1 medium-large egg
- 1 teaspoon dried oregano
- 1 tablespoon olive oil
- 1/2 teaspoon ground cumin
- 1/2 teaspoon ground coriander
- 1/2 a cup breadcrumbs
- flour for dredging
- oil for frying
- salt and freshly ground pepper to taste
- 1 tablespoon finely grated Greek kefalotyri cheese or good-quality pecorino or Parmigiano-Reggiano (optional)

Method:

1. To start this traditional Greek lamb meatballs recipe (arnisioi keftedes), add all the ingredients into a big bowl and mix, squeeze with your hands, to allow the flavors to blend. Cover the bowl with some plastic wrap and let it rest in the fridge for at least 15 minutes.
2. To make the Greek lamb meatballs, roll the mixture into balls, about the size of a walnut. Dredge lightly each meatball in flour, until well covered. Move to a plate, shaking off any excess flour.
3. Cooking Greek lamb meatballs, the traditional way is to fry them in a lot of oil.

4. To fry Greek lamb meatballs, use a large, deep frying pan and pour in the oil to a depth of about 1/2 an inch (1,5 cm). Heat the oil over medium-high heat until it begins to boil. Add the lamb meatballs in batches in a single layer and fry for about 7 minutes, turning occasionally, until browned and crisp on all sides. Using a slotted spoon, remove the meatballs to a plate lined with paper.

5. If you prefer a lighter version, you can bake/ grill the meatballs. Preheat the oven at 200C, place the lamb meatballs on greased baking sheet about an inch apart. Bake for about 20 minutes, turning the meatballs upside down midway through cooking time.

6. Greek lamb meatballs are ideally served as an appetizer (meze) with some creamy tzatziki sauce and pita breads or as a main course with some basmati rice and a Greek salad. Enjoy!

Kakavia (Fisherman's Soup)

Serves: 6

Ingredients:

- 1kg hake steaks on the bone (plus a hake head, about 400g)
- 400g cyprus potatoes (cut into 3cm chunks)
- 400ml extra-virgin olive oil
- 250g carrots (finely chopped)
- 200g celery (finely sliced)
- 200g ripe tomatoes (roughly chopped) 150g fennel bulb (trimmed and chopped, fronds reserved)
- 200ml freshly squeezed lemon juice (plus wedges to serve)
- 1 tablespoon roughly ground fennel seeds
- Small bunch fresh parsley (roughly chopped, to serve)
- Barley rusks or sourdough bread to serve

Method:

1. Prepare a large pan with a lid and put the potatoes in (they should fit snugly in a single layer). Add the fennel, carrots, celery and tomatoes on top. Add the fish head and the fennel seeds and a dash of salt. Pour in the olive oil and 1-liter water, then put over a high heat.
2. Cover with a lid and bring the soup to the boil, then cook over a high heat for about 25-30 minutes, shaking the pan regularly to prevent sticking.
3. Using a slotted spoon, remove the fish head. Add the hake steaks to the pan with the lemon juice and cook for about 5 minutes, then turn off the heat. Taste and season. Let the soup sit before serving – it's not supposed to be eaten piping hot. Use a fork to flake the hake off the bone.

Scatter with the parsley and reserved fennel fronds, then serve with lemon wedges and rusks or crusty bread.

Kotosoupa Avgolemono (Greek Lemon Chicken Soup)

Serves: 3-4

Ingredients:

- 1 chicken (1- 1.2 kg/35-40 ounces)
- 150-200g (6-7 ounces) short-grain rice like Arborio
- 5 cups of water
- 2 medium-large eggs
- 1 red onion (peeled)
- 1 lemon (juiced)
- salt and freshly ground pepper to taste
- 2 carrots (optional)

Method:

1. To start this traditional Greek lemon chicken soup, clean thoroughly the chicken in running water and place in a deep pan. Press the chicken with your hands down to the bottom of the pan, add the onion, whole (and the carrot), pour in the water (the water should cover the chicken) and season. Place on high heat, put the lid on and bring to the boil; turn the heat down and boil the chicken for about 1 hour and 15 minutes (the chicken is ready, when the meat can be removed easily from the bones). While the chicken boils, some white foam will probably surface on the water. Remove that foam with a slotted spoon.
2. Take out the chicken from the broth and strain the broth. Add the hot broth in a pan, add the rice and season with salt and pepper and boil, until done.
3. Pull the meat from the bones and discard the skin when the chicken is cool enough to handle. Dice the meat into bites.
4. For the egg lemon sauce, break the eggs into a bowl and whisk, until foamy; add the lemon juice and whisk again.

Add into the bowl a ladle of hot soup and whisk quickly. Add one more ladle and whisk again, so that the eggs get warm. Pour the egg mixture back into the pot, whilst constantly stirring, put the lid on and leave for about 3-4 minutes.

5. Serve while still warm; ladle into bowls, top with the diced chicken and sprinkle with freshly ground pepper or paprika. Enjoy!

Magiritsa

Serves: 3-4

Ingredients:

- 1 kg lamb offal (heart, liver, lungs and other organs)
- 5-6 spring onions (finely chopped)
- 4-5 tablespoons fresh dill (chopped)
- 3 medium-large romaine lettuce (roughly chopped)
- 1 medium-large red onion (finely chopped)
- 1/2 cup rice (optional)
- 1/2 a cup olive oil
- salt and freshly ground pepper
- intestines from 1 lamb (optional)

For the egg lemon sauce (Avgolemono):

- 2 medium-large eggs
- 2 lemons (juiced)

Method:

1. To start, clean and wash the organs thoroughly and set aside. Wash thoroughly the intestines under running water, rub them with sea salt and lemon juice and wash again. (To wash them more easily you can either slice them up lengthwise or turn them inside out.)
2. In a big pot, add the organs and plenty of water and bring to the boil. Blanch the organs in the hot water for about 3-5 minutes. Add the intestines and blanch for 5 more minutes. Drain and set aside to cool down for a while. Chop in small pieces and remove the excessive fat.
3. Heat a large pot over medium-high heat and add the olive oil, the chopped onions and the meat. Sauté for 5-6 minutes, until browned. Add 2-3 glasses of hot water and simmer for about 10 minutes. Add the roughly chopped

lettuce squeezing them down to fit and place the lid on. Cook for 10 minutes, remove the lid and season. Stir well and cook the magiritsa with the lid on for about 40-50 more minutes. (If you choose to make this magiritsa recipe with rice, stir in the rice about 10 minutes before the end of cooking time.)

4. Prepare the egg lemon sauce for the magiritsa. Start by separating the egg whites from the egg yolks. In a bowl, whisk the egg yolks and add the lemon juice whist whisking until combined. In another bowl add the egg whites and whisk using a hand mixer until the egg whites are foamy and thick. While whisking slowly add the yolk mixture in the egg whites. Continue whisking for 1-2 minutes and gradually add 1-2 ladles of the hot broth from the magiritsa, a little bit at a time. Make sure you add the broth slowly or the egg whites will curdle! When done, pour the mixture back into the pot and add the chopped dill. Stir well, place the lid on and leave aside for 5 minutes. (See also some tips to make the perfect Avgolemono).

5. Ladle the magiritsa (Greek Easter soup) while still warm into bowls and sprinkle with freshly ground pepper. Enjoy!

Psarosoupa (Greek Style Fish Soup)

Serves: 4-6

Ingredients:

- 600g fish fillets (red mullet, snapper, cod)
- 120 ml olive oil
- 10 whole peppercorns
- 6 cups (1.25 liters) water
- 5-6 parsley stalks
- 3 medium-large carrots (cut into even chunks approx. 2cm each)
- 2 medium-large potatoes (cut into even chunks approx. 2cm each)
- 2 stalks of celery (cut into even chunks approx. 2cm each)
- 1 leek (finely sliced)
- 1 red onion (cut into eighths)
- 1 teaspoon salt
- 1 lemon (juiced)
- freshly chopped parsley (garnish)

Method:

1. Combine the carrots, celery, leek, onions, potatoes, peppercorns and parsley stalks along with the water in a large pot over a medium-high heat. Season with salt and allow the mixture to come to boil and then simmer it on a low heat for approx. 20mins until the carrots and potatoes are just tender.
2. Pour the stock in a new pot and strain the veggies using a fine sieve and place them on a plate discarding the peppercorns and parsley stalks.

3. Place half the veggies back into the stock and mash roughly with a fork. Add the olive oil and fish fillets and allow the soup to come to a boil.
4. Simmer for 20-30 mins depending on how thick your fish fillets are and add the lemon juice. Stir and remove from the heat.
5. Place cooked veggies and fish pieces along with the soup in individual bowls and serve immediately garnished with freshly chopped parsley.

Trahana Soup with Lemon and Olive Oil

Serves: 6

Ingredients:

- 8 cups water (vegetable stock or chicken stock)
- 6 tablespoons crumbled feta
- 3 tablespoons extra virgin olive oil
- 3 tablespoons lemon juice, strained
- 1 1/2 cups sour bulgur trahana
- chopped fresh herbs (garnish)
- salt and freshly ground pepper to taste
- plain Greek yogurt for garnish (optional)

Method:

1. Heat 2 tablespoons of olive oil in a medium soup pot over medium heat and add trahana. Stir until coated with oil, about 1 minute.
2. Add water or stock and bring to a boil. Add salt and pepper to taste, reduce the heat and simmer, stirring often, until trahana is tender and nutty tasting and the broth slightly thickened, 15 to 20 minutes if using home-made bulgur trahana (if you use semolina or flour trahana the time will only be 8 to 12 minutes and the mixture will be more like a porridge).
3. Remove from heat and stir in lemon juice. Spoon into bowls and top with a drizzle of olive oil and a tablespoon of crumbled feta. Garnish with plain yogurt if desired and chopped fresh herbs such as mint, parsley or dill.

Bourdeto (Fish recipe from Corfu)

Serves: 3

Ingredients:

- 4 medium-large fish fillets
- 1 medium-large beef tomato (skinned and chopped)
- 1 red onion (chopped)
- 1/2 carton passata
- 1/2 lemon (juiced)
- chili powder
- some parsley (chopped)
- extra virgin olive oil

Method:

1. In a frying pan, add the olive oil and sauté the onion for a minute until soft. Add the tomato, passata, salt, pepper, chili powder, and a little hot water and simmer for 15 minutes. Add the fish (if using fillet, it must be defrosted and washed). Add hot water, if needed, to half-cover the fish.
2. Simmer uncovered for 10-15 minutes. Check occasionally to make sure fish is covered with the sauce. Turn over gently if using whole fish, or spoon sauce from the pan over the fish every now and then to make sure it's covered fully and staying moist.
3. Taste to check fish is done, add salt if needed. When sauce has thickened, add chopped parsley and lemon juice and move the pan gently in your hands to spread the lemon juice and the sauce evenly. Cover, switch off heat and leave it on the hob for another minute, then serve immediately with fries, fresh bread and a salad.

Giouvetsi (Greek Beef stew with Orzo pasta)

Serves: 3-4

Ingredients:

- 1 kg (35 ounces) veal shoulder (cut into portions)
- 250g (9 ounces) orzo pasta (kritharaki/manestra)
- 100g (5 ounces) grated kefalotyri or feta cheese
- 2 medium-large red onions (finely chopped)
- 2 medium carrots (sliced about 1 cm thick)
- 2 tablespoons tomato puree
- 1 tin of chopped tomatoes
- 1 teaspoon sugar
- 1 glass of red wine
- 1 cinnamon stick
- 1/2 cup of olive oil

Method:

1. Use paper towels to wipe the meat. Heat 1/2 of a cup of olive oil into a frying pan, add the chopped onions and carrots and sauté for 5 minutes in medium-low heat. Turn up the heat and add the veal; brown the meat on all sides until crusty.
2. Stir in the tomato purée and pour in the red wine; wait for the wine to evaporate. Add the tinned tomatoes, a glass of water, the sugar, the cinnamon stick and a good pinch of salt and pepper.
3. Turn the heat down and simmer with the lid on for about 45 minutes.
4. Heat another pan, add 3 tablespoon of olive oil and the orzo pasta and sauté until golden.
5. Put the orzo pasta in an oven tray along with the meat and sauce (remove the cinnamon stick) and mix. Cover the tray with some aluminum foil and bake in preheated

oven at 180C for 30 minutes. Remove the aluminum foil, add a glass of water if needed, and put back in the oven for another 15 minutes.

6. Sprinkle with some grated kefalotyri or any hard-yellow cheese and enjoy!

Traditional Sofrito Recipe from Corfu

Serves: 3-4

Ingredients:

- 1 kg (35 oz./2 pounds) top round boneless veal (cut in 6 slices)
- 150g (5 oz.) all-purpose flour (for dredging)
- 7-9 cloves of garlic (sliced)
- 1 and 2/3 cups beef broth (warm)
- 1/2 a cup fresh parsley (chopped)
- 1 tablespoon butter
- 1/3 of a cup olive oil (for frying)
- 1/3 of a cup white wine vinegar
- 1/3 of a cup white wine
- salt and freshly ground pepper to taste

Method:

1. Start by preparing the veal. Season the meat with salt and freshly ground pepper and dredge lightly the veal slices with flour, tapping off any excess.
2. Heat the oil and butter in a large nonstick skillet over medium-high heat. Add the veal (in batches) and sauté, until browned on all sides. Do not add all the meat in the sauce pan, rather sauté in batches, so that the temperature of the oil remains high and the meat is sealed. When done, remove with a slotted spoon, place on a platter, cover and set aside.
3. Cut the garlic cloves in slices and add in the same oil used to brown the meat. Turn down to medium heat and stir for a minute. Pour in the white wine vinegar and deglaze. Add the veal and the white wine and wait for a couple of minutes to steam up. Add the warm broth and season with salt and pepper.

4. Turn the heat down to low-medium and simmer until the veal is tender and the sauce thickens, for about 30-40 minutes. About 5 minutes before removing from the heat, stir in the freshly chopped parsley.
5. Serve the Sofrito while still hot over mashed potatoes, rice or fries, with some crusted garlic bread aside. Enjoy!

Pilafi (Lemony Greek Rice Pilaf with Chicken Thighs)

Serves: 6-8

Ingredients:

- 8 chicken thighs (bone-in and skin on)
- 6-7 peppercorns
- 3 cups chicken stock
- 2-3 tablespoons olive oil
- 2 tablespoons butter
- 1 1/2 cup rice (long grain rice or basmati)
- 1 small red onion (roughly chopped)
- 1 lemon (juiced, more if you prefer)
- salt and freshly ground pepper
- 150g/5 oz. feta cheese for garnish (optional)

Method:

1. Start by washing the chicken thighs thoroughly and pat them dry with some paper towel. Drizzle the chicken thighs with olive oil, season well with salt and pepper and rub using your hands.
2. Place the chicken thighs in a large pan over medium-high heat. Let them color and cook for about 6 minutes on each side, until the skin is nicely colored and crispy. Remove the chicken thighs from the pan and set side.
3. Start to prepare the Greek rice pilaf. In the same pan add 1-2 tablespoons olive oil and the chopped onions and sauté until soft. Add the butter and rice and sauté the rice until soft. Pour in the chicken stock and lemon juice and deglaze. Add the chicken thighs (skin side up) and season well with salt and pepper.
4. Place the lid on, turn the heat down and simmer the Greek rice pilaf for about 15 minutes, until the chicken and rice are cooked and all the liquid has been absorbed.

5. Finish off the Greek rice pilaf with a last-minute squeeze of lemon juice, crumbled feta cheese and freshly ground pepper. Enjoy!

Brizola sto Fourno (Greek Pork Chops Recipe with Roast Potatoes)

Serves: 4

Ingredients:

- 4 pork chops (bone-in, approx. 2.5 cm thick)
- 7 medium-large potatoes (cut in wedges)

For the marinade:

- 2 cloves of garlic (sliced)
- 1 tablespoon red wine vinegar
- 1 red onion (roughly chopped)
- 1 tablespoon dried oregano
- 1/3 of a cup olive oil
- salt and freshly ground pepper to taste
- 1 tablespoon mustard (optional)

For the potatoes:

- 2 tablespoons olive oil
- 1 clove of garlic (minced)
- 1 teaspoon dried oregano
- 1/4 of cup dry white wine
- 1/2 lemon (juiced)
- salt and freshly ground pepper to taste

Method:

1. Start by preparing the marinade. In a big bowl, add the roughly chopped onions, the garlic slices and the pork chops (brizola). Drizzle with olive oil and red wine vinegar and season with salt and freshly ground pepper. Sprinkle the pork chops with oregano and blend to coat.

69

Cover the bowl with plastic wrap, chill and let marinade for 1-2 hours.

2. Cut a big piece of parchment paper and soak it with water. Squeeze to get rid of the excessive water and line on a large baking tray. Place the potatoes on the parchment paper, drizzle with olive oil and lemon juice, pour in the white wine and season with salt. Sprinkle the potatoes with oregano and minced garlic. Cover with a large wet piece of parchment paper and join the edges together to seal. Bake at 180C for about 45 minutes.

3. Now it's time to get some color on the pork chops. Heat a griddle pan over high heat and sear the pork chops for about 1 minute on each side, until nicely colored.

4. Turn the baking tray out of the oven. Uncover the parchment paper and place the pork chops over the potatoes on a single layer. Cover again to seal and pop back in the oven for about 10-15 minutes, depending on the thickness of the pork chops.

5. Remove the baking tray from the oven, unwrap and remove the pork chops. Cover the pork chops with aluminum foil and let rest for 10 minutes. Bake the potatoes uncovered for about 15 minutes, until nicely colored.

6. Serve while still warm.

Lamb Kleftiko (Greek Lamb Cooked In Parchment Paper)

Serves: 6-8

Ingredients:

- 1-1.2 kg/ 35 oz. leg of lamb, boneless (approx. 2kg/ 70 oz. bone in)
- 200g (7 oz.) kefalotyri or Graviera or any had yellow cheese (cut into cubes)
- 5 medium-large potatoes
- 4 cloves of garlic (2 sliced and 2 whole)
- 2-3 bell peppers (green, red, orange)
- 2 small-medium red onions
- 2 tablespoons mustard
- 1 tablespoon dried oregano
- 1/2 lemon (juiced)
- 1/2 a cup olive oil
- 1/2 a cup dry white wine
- 1/2 ripe tomato (sliced)
- parchment paper
- kitchen string
- salt and freshly ground pepper to taste

Method:

1. Start by washing thoroughly the lamb and cut into portions (approx. 5*6 cm). Place in a large bowl or basin and set aside.
2. How to prepare the vegetables for the lamb kleftiko; Cut the onions in half and then in four wedges. Cut the peppers in 2-3 cm chunks and slice 2 cloves of garlic. Add the vegetables in the bowl with the lamb and pour in the olive oil, white wine and lemon juice. Add the mustard, 2 whole cloves of garlic, sprinkle with oregano and season

with salt and pepper. Use your hands to blend all the ingredients together.

3. Cover the bowl with plastic wrap, chill and let marinade for at least 2 hours. It's best to leave the meat for the lamb kleftiko marinade overnight, to soak up all the fantastic flavors.

4. Once the meat for the lamb kleftiko is marinated, return the lamb at room temperature. In the same bowl add the cheese (cut into 2cm cubes) and blend. Preheat the oven to 180C.

5. To prepare the potatoes, peel the potatoes and cut in four pieces. (The lamb kleftiko will require about 2 1/2 hours baking, so it's best to cut the potatoes in large pieces, to keep their shape.)

6. Now it's time to wrap the lamb kleftiko in parchment paper. Lay 4 long pieces of parchment paper to form a star. Pop the potatoes in the center of the parchment paper and season with salt and a pinch of oregano. Pour the marinade from the lamb over the potatoes and set the lamb and vegetables on top of the potatoes. Layer with the sliced tomato and enclose the lamb kleftiko into a pouch. To enclose the lamb kleftiko hold the parchment paper from the edges, crosswise and grab with your hand in the middle, just above the stuffing and squeeze. Use the kitchen string to tie tightly the whole thing together, just above the stuffing and lift into a roasting tin.

7. Roast the lamb kleftiko in the oven for about 1 hour 45 minutes until tender. Remove the tin from the oven and increase the temperature to 220C. Unwrap the lamb kleftiko and scrunch the parchment paper under the rim of the tin. Baste the lamb with the juices and return in the oven for a further 20 mins until browned. Remove the pieces of lamb from the pouch and wrap them in some foil to rest. Toss the potatoes and return in the oven for about 20 minutes, until nicely colored.

8. Return the lamb pieces in the roasting tin and serve the lamb kleftiko as it is. Enjoy!

Chapter Three: Greek Dinner Recipes

Greek Lamb Souvlaki

Serves: 8-10

Ingredients:

- 1kg (35 oz.) lamb leg or shoulder (cut into chunks)
- 80ml (approx. 5-6 tablespoon) olive oil
- 10 metal or wooden skewers
- 2 red onions (roughly chopped)
- 2 cloves of garlic (crushed)
- 1 lemon (juiced)
- 1 teaspoon dried Greek oregano
- 1 teaspoon dried thyme or some fresh thyme (chopped)
- salt and freshly ground pepper
- 1/2 teaspoon smoked sweet paprika (optional)
- 1/2 teaspoon cumin (optional)

For the tzatziki sauce:

- 500g (18 ounces) of strained yogurt
- 2 cloves of garlic (minced)
- 1-2 tablespoons of red wine vinegar
- 1 cucumber
- 1/4 of a cup extra virgin olive oil
- a dash of salt

To serve:

- 10 pita breads
- 1 teaspoon dried oregano
- olive oil
- salt to taste

Method:

1. To start, cut the meat into equal sized (3 cm) chunks and set aside.
2. To prepare the marinade, in a large bowl add the olive oil, garlic, lemon juice, the herbs and spices and season with freshly ground pepper – don't add salt yet. Whisk all the ingredients to combine. Add the meat and the chopped onions and blend to coat. Cover the bowl with plastic wrap, chill and let marinade for at least 4 hours. It's best to leave the meat for the lamb souvlaki marinade overnight, to soak up all the wonderful flavors. (If you are at home blend the marinade once in a while).
3. While you wait, prepare the tzatziki sauce for the lamb souvlaki. Pour in a blender the olive oil and grated garlic and blend until combined. Remove the skin and the seeds of the cucumber and grate it into a large bowl. Season with salt and pepper and leave aside for 10 minutes. Wrap the grated cucumber in a towel and squeeze, in order to get rid of the excess water. In a bowl, add the cucumber, the blended garlic and oil, the yogurt, 1-2 tbsps of red wine vinegar, a pinch of salt and blend, until the ingredients are combined. Store the tzatziki sauce in the fridge and always serve cold.
4. To make the lamb souvlaki (skewers), you can either use wooden or metal skewers. For this lamb souvlaki recipe, you will need about 10 skewers, depending on the size of each lamb souvlaki. If using wooden skewers, cut them to fit your griddle pan and soak them in water. (This will prevent them from burning.) Lift the chunks of lamb out of the marinade and thread the pieces, comfortably, on the skewers. At this point don't forget to season your lamb souvlaki with salt.
5. Heat a grill, barbecue or griddle pan and cook the lamb souvlaki for about 10-15 minutes, until cooked to your liking.

6. While your lamb souvlaki is cooking, prepare the pita breads. Preheat the oven to 250C. Use a cooking brush to lightly oil the pita breads on both sides and season with salt and oregano. Place a large oven tray at the bottom of the oven and place the pita breads on top of the tray. Bake for 2-3 minutes. (Alternatively barbecue the pita breads, until nicely coloured on both sides).
7. Enjoy this delicious Greek lamb souvlaki recipe with pita bread and tzatziki sauce with a nice refreshing Greek feta salad.

Octopus Stifado (Greek Octopus and Onion Stew)

Serves: 3-4

Ingredients:

- 1 large octopus (approx. 1 kg/35 oz; cleaned)
- 1 kg (35 oz.) baby shallot onions (peeled)
- 2 tablespoons red wine vinegar
- 3-4 allspice berries
- 2 cloves of garlic (chopped)
- 2 tablespoons tomato paste
- 2 bay leaves
- 1 glass red wine
- 1/2 red onion (grated)
- 1/3 of a cup olive oil
- salt and pepper to taste

Method:

1. To prepare, place the octopus in a large pot, pour in 1 cup of water and the vinegar. Boil the octopus for about 20 minutes. Remove the octopus from the pan, chop into pieces and place in a bowl along with 1 cup of the broth.
2. In the meantime, peel the shallots and carve them crosswise. A little trick to peel them more easily is to place the shallots in a bowl full of water and leave them in the fridge overnight.
3. In a medium saucepan add the oil and shallots (whole) and sauté (medium heat) for about 10 minutes or until softened. Turn the heat up, add the octopus and sauté. Add the tomato paste, grated onion and garlic and sauté for 1 more minute.
4. Pour in the red wine, 1 cup of the hot broth, the bay leaves, allspice berries and season. Bring to a boil, turn the heat down and let the octopus stifado simmer for

about 30-40 minutes, or until the octopus is tender and the sauce has thickened. If the sauce needs some more thickening, then let it cook for a while uncovered.

Patates Yahni (Country-style Greek Potato Stew)

Serves: 3-4

Ingredients:

- 8 medium-large potatoes (peeled and cut into 2.5 cm chunks)
- 3 medium ripe tomatoes (peeled and grated)
- 2 cloves of garlic (finely chopped)
- 1 medium-large red onion (finely chopped)
- 1 tablespoon tomato paste
- 1 tablespoon salt
- 3/4 of a cup olive oil
- 1/2 teaspoon freshly ground pepper
- 2-3 tablespoon schopped parsley

Method:

1. Start by preparing your vegetables. Peel and cut the potatoes into 2.5 cm chunks, finely chop (or grate) the onion and garlic and set aside. Peel the tomatoes and grate. You may find it easier to peel the tomatoes if you blanch them first for 1 minute in hot water. (For this Greek potato stew recipe, it is best to use fresh tomatoes rather than canned.)
2. Heat a big pot over medium-high heat. Add the olive oil and onion and sauté until softened. Stir in the garlic and sauté for 1 more minute. Add the tomato paste and cook for 1 more minute.
3. In the same pot add the grated tomatoes, the potatoes, sprinkle with chopped parsley and season with salt and pepper. Add just enough warm water to cover the potatoes (whilst stirring occasionally) and bring to the boil. Turn the heat down to medium, cover and simmer for 30 minutes or until the potatoes are tender.

4. Greek potato stew (Patates Yahni) is best served while still warm or at room temperature. Enjoy!

Giouvarlakia/Youvarlakia (Traditional Greek Meatball Soup in Egg-Lemon Sauce)

Serves: 4-5

Ingredients:

For the meatballs:

- 500g (18 ounces) lean minced beef
- 2 tablespoons olive oil
- 1 medium sized onion (finely chopped)
- 1 medium egg
- 1 teaspoon salt
- ½ cup parsley (finely chopped)
- ¼ of a cup long-grain rice (not boiled)
- a pinch of coriander
- freshly ground pepper
- ½ carrot, grated (optional)
- 3 tablespoons fresh dill, finely chopped (optional)

For the egg lemon sauce:

- 2 medium eggs
- 2 lemons (juiced)
- 1 tablespoons flour

Method:

1. Put the pork shank in a big pot, add water, salt, bay leaf, peeled garlic cloves, dark pepper and allspice corns. Take it to a boil, and over low heat, cook for about 2-2,5 hours or until soft.
2. In the meantime, boil potatoes with their skin on in somewhat salted water until fifty percent done. Peel them, slice into quarters and place in a roasting skillet greased with oil.

3. Preheat the oven to 200 °C. Remove the shank from water and put on the potato bed. Add peeled shallots or sliced up onions and 1-2 ladles of the cooking food liquid, sprinkle salt and caraway seeds on the meats and vegetables. Put in place the oven and roast for approximately 30-35 minutes until it turns brownish.
4. Serve with pickles.

Briam (Greek mixed Roasted Vegetables)

Serves: 6-8

Ingredients:

- 1 kg (35 oz.) ripe medium tomatoes (peeled and sliced)
- 1/2 kg (18 oz.) aubergines (sliced)
- 1/2 kg (18 oz.) potatoes (sliced)
- 1/2 kg (18 oz.) courgette (sliced)
- 2 cloves of garlic (finely chopped)
- 2 tablespoons chopped parsley
- 1 red onion (sliced)
- 3/4 of a cup olive oil
- salt and freshly ground pepper to taste

Method:

1. Start by preparing the vegetables. Peel and cut the potatoes in slices. Wash thoroughly the courgettes and aubergines and slice into 1cm slices. Alternatively, you can cut the vegetables in chunks. Peel the tomatoes and cut into thin slices. (You can also use green bell peppers).
2. Use a large baking pan to bake the briam, approx. 30*35cm, so that the vegetables are not layered too deep.
3. Layer the bottom of the pan with sliced tomatoes and season. Place on top the sliced vegetables and season well. Sprinkle with the onion and garlic and top with the rest of the tomatoes. Season well, garnish with chopped parsley and drizzle with olive oil.
4. Put aluminum foil to cover the briam and bake in preheated oven at 200C (both top and bottom heating elements on) for 1 1/2 to 2 hours. Uncover the briam halfway through cooking time, toss the vegetables and continue baking until nicely coloured.

5. Serve this traditional briam dish with salty feta cheese and lots of bread. Enjoy!

Kalamarakia Tiganita (Crispy Fried Calamari)

Serves: 6-8

Ingredients:

- 700g (25 oz.) calamari
- 100g (3.5 oz.) bread flour
- 50g (1.5 oz.) semolina flour (1.5 oz.)
- 2 tablespoons salt
- 1 tablespoon peppercorns (or grounded pepper)
- 1 tablespoon oregano (optional)
- 1/2 tablespoon paprika (optional)
- vegetable oil for frying

Method:

1. Start by cleaning the calamari under running water and wash thoroughly. Using a sharp knife cut the calamari in slices, approx. 1 cm each. This will create the rings, as seen in the picture below. Place the calamari rings on some paper towel to remove of the excessive water.
2. For the seasoning, add the seasoning and pulse into a blender until powdered. (Alternatively, you can use a pestle.)
3. In a large sandwich bag or tupperware add the flour and seasoning. Place in the sliced calamari and shake well to coat (you will need to do this in batches). Remove the calamari onto a plate, shaking of any excess flour.
4. Put into a medium sized frying pan pour enough vegetable oil to deep fry the calamari. Heat the oil to medium high heat until it begins to bubble. Test if the oil is hot enough by dipping one of the calamari rings in; if it sizzles the oil is ready. Fry the calamari in batches for about 2-3 minutes, until nicely golden.

5. Remove the fried calamari using a slotted spoon and place on some paper towel to dry for 1-2 minutes. Have a taste and sprinkle with some more salt.
6. Enjoy these delicious Greek fried calamari recipe with a squeeze of a lemon.

Greek Kolokithopita (Traditional Zucchini Pie with Feta Cheese)

Serves: 6-8

Ingredients:

For the filling:

- 1kg (35 oz.) zucchini (grated)
- 500g (17 oz.) feta cheese (crumbled)
- 200g (7 oz.) strained Greek yogurt
- 4-5 tablespoons powdered melba toast
- 4-5 leaves fresh mint (chopped)
- 2 tablespoons parsley (chopped)
- 2 tablespoons olive oil
- 2 medium-large eggs
- 1 red onion (finely chopped)
- salt and freshly ground pepper to taste

For the dough:

- 500g (18 oz.) all-purpose flour
- 200-250g (3/4 – 1 cup) water
- 90g (1/3 of a cup) olive oil
- 2 tablespoons red wine vinegar
- 1 1/2 teaspoon salt

Method:

1. Start by making the dough. In a large mixing bowl add the flour and salt, make a well in the center and pour in the vinegar and olive oil. Use a dough hook mix to combine the ingredients for 10-15 seconds. (Tip: The vinegar helps the dough for the zucchini pie to become crispy.)

2. Depending on the kind of flour, the weather, the humidity and various factors, the dough for the zucchini pie may need a little bit more or less water than this recipe calls for. Start by adding 200g of water at first (3/4 of a cup) and mix, until the flour absorbs the water. After mixing for a while, the dough should become an elastic ball. The perfect dough for your zucchini pie should be soft, malleable and smooth. If the dough is still crumbled, then you need to add a little bit more water. Add a few drops of water and mix for a while. Check out the consistency of your dough and add a few more drops of water, if needed. In case you added more water than needed, the dough will become sticky. Don't worry, you can fix that by adding some more flour (add 1/2 teaspoon at first, mix and check again).

3. When you are happy with the consistency of the dough for your zucchini pie, wrap with some plastic wrap and let the dough rest for 45-60 minutes. This is essential, so that the dough softens and you can roll it easily.

4. In the meantime, prepare the filling for the zucchini pie (Greek kolokithopita). Remove the skin of the zucchinis and grate them into a colander, season with salt and leave aside for 20 minutes to drain. Wrap the grated zucchinis in a towel and squeeze, in order to get rid of the excess water. In a saucepan add 2 tablespoons olive oil and sauté the onions, until soft. Add all the ingredients for the filling of the zucchini pie in a large bowl and blend to combine. Set aside.

5. For this zucchini pie recipe, you will need a large baking pan approx. 25x35cm. Using a cooking brush oil, the bottom and sides of the pan.

6. Divide the dough into two halves. You will use half the dough for the bottom of the zucchini pie and the other half to cover it. Place half the dough on a floured surface and coat your rolling pin with some flour. Make a circle of dough with your hands; now you are ready to roll!

Ensure that your dough has plenty of flour to prevent it from sticking to the working surface or the rolling pin. At first, roll out a few times, turning the dough every once in a while, to keep the circle even and the dough from sticking to the surface. Gently roll the edge of the dough over the rolling pin and roll the dough around the pin. Place your hands in the center of the rolling pin and as you roll, move them out to the sides so that both the rolling pin and your hands are working to spread and thin the dough. Unroll, turn a half turn and repeat. Continue rolling making the dough thinner and thinner each time. Move your hands from the center to the sides to keep even pressure and help in spreading and thinning the dough. Carefully roll your dough around the rolling pin and then unroll it over the pan and ease the dough into the dish, pushing it into all sides.

7. Tip in the filling of the zucchini pie. Roll out the rest of the dough, roll your dough around the rolling pin and then unroll it over the filling of the zucchini pie (kolokithopita). With a knife trim some of the excessive phyllo and roll the rest on the edges. Brush the top with enough olive oil and make some holes on top of the zucchini pie with a sharp knife. Drizzle the kolokithopita with some water and sprinkle with sesame seeds.

8. Bake the zucchini pie in preheated oven at 180C for 50-60 minutes, until nicely colored.

9. Serve this delicious Greek zucchini pie (kolokithopita) as starter, mid-day snack or as a main dish with a nice Greek feta salad aside. Enjoy!

Spanakorizo (Greek Spinach and Rice)

Serves: 6-8

Ingredients:

- 1kg spinach (35 oz.), rinsed and stemmed
- 200g rice (7 oz.) white rice
- 4 spring onions (chopped)
- 1 red onion (finely chopped)
- 1 leek (sliced)
- 1/2 cup olive oil
- 1/2 bunch dill (finely chopped)
- salt and freshly ground pepper
- 150g tinned chopped tomatoes (5.5 oz.) or 200g of fresh tomatoes, if in season (optional)
- 1 tablespoon tomato paste (optional)

Method:

1. Start by heating the olive oil in a large pan over medium high heat. Add the onions, spring onions and leek and sauté for 3-4 minutes, until translucent.
2. Add the spinach and cook stirring for a few minutes, until wilted. Stir in the tomatoes, the tomato paste, a glass of hot water, the rice and season. Reduce heat to low and simmer for about 20-25 minutes, until the rice is tender.
3. During cooking, stir the spanakorizo once in a while and check if the pan appears to be getting dry, and add some more hot water, if needed. Finish the spanakorizo with fresh chopped dill and cook for a few more minutes.
4. Serve with a squeeze of a lemon and top with crumbled feta.

Fasolada (Traditional Greek Bean Soup)

Serves: 3-4

Ingredients:

- 500g (18 ounces) dry white beans
- 130ml (1/2 cup) extra virgin olive oil
- 3-4 carrots (finely chopped)
- 3 stalks of celery (finely chopped)
- 2 tablespoons tomato puree
- 1 large red onion (finely chopped)
- a dash of paprika (hot or sweet, your choice)
- salt and freshly ground pepper to taste

Method:

1. Place the beans in a medium saucepan with plenty of cold water to cover them. Bring to the boil, turn the heat down to medium and parboil for 30-35 minutes, until slightly tender. Drain in colander and set aside.
2. Finely chop the onion, celery and carrots. Add 3-4 tablespoons of olive oil in a deep pan, add the chopped vegetables and blend. Sauté for about 2 minutes and add the tomato paste and continue sautéing for a minute.
3. Add the parboiled beans in the pan and pour in enough boiling water to cover the beans and little bit more and blend lightly. Place the lid on and simmer the fasolada for about 35 minutes, until the beans are tender.
4. Towards the end of cooking time, pour in the remaining olive oil and season with salt and pepper. Boil for a few more minutes, until the soup becomes thick and creamy.
5. Serve while still steaming hot with a few Kalamata olives and of course some village bread. Enjoy!

Prasopita (Traditional Greek Leek Pie)

Serves: 8-10

Ingredients:

- 800-900 g (28 oz.) leeks (sliced)
- 250ml (1 cup) milk or milk cream
- 150g (5 oz.) feta cheese (crumbled)
- 100g (3.5 oz.) Graviera cheese (or hard yellow cheese)
- 12-15 phyllo sheets (thawed)
- 1 egg and 1 teaspoon water to brush the top
- 1 medium-large egg yolk
- 3-4 spring onions (finely chopped)
- 1/2 a glass white wine
- olive oil or butter for brushing the pan
- salt and pepper to taste

Method:

1. If you're making this Greek leek pie with commercial phyllo dough, it is important to thaw the phyllo dough completely by putting it in the fridge from the previous day. For the beginners at working with phyllo, check the handling tips before starting.
2. Start by making the filling. Wash the leeks and trim them, keeping only the white part and cut in slices (2cm width).
3. Heat a saucepan and add olive oil, the leeks and scallions and season with salt and pepper. Sauté until tender while stirring. Deglaze with the white wine and wait for it to evaporate. Remove the pan from the stove and allow them to cool down for a while.

4. In a bowl, add 1 egg yolk and the milk cream and whisk. Stir in the leek's mixture, feta cheese, graviera cheese, season with pepper and blend to combine.
5. Brush a medium sized baking tray with olive oil and lay one sheet of phyllo dough, allowing it to exceed the pan. Brush the phyllo sheet with olive oil or melted butter and continue with 5-6 more phyllo sheets (brushing each one with olive oil or melted butter). Tip in the filling and even out using a spatula. With a knife trim some of the excessive phyllo, and fold the excess phyllo sheets flaps over the mixture. Add 5-6 more phyllo sheets, making sure to oil or butter each one, before adding the other. Trim some of the excessive phyllo and roll the rest on the edges.
6. In a bowl whisk the egg and the water, brush the top of the leek pie and scar into pieces. Bake in preheated oven at 180C for about 50 minutes, until nicely colored.
7. Enjoy this traditional vegetarian Greek leek pie as a filling snack or as light meal.

Giouvetsi Kotopoulo (Chicken with Orzo Pasta)

Serves: 3-4

Ingredients:

- 550-600g (20 ounces) boneless skinless chicken breasts (cut into bites)
- 130g (4.5 ounces) feta cheese (crumbled)
- 4 tablespoons olive oil
- 2 cups of water
- 1 1/2 cup orzo pasta (kritharaki/manestra)
- 1 small red onion (finely chopped)
- 1 teaspoon tomato paste
- 1/2 tin chopped tomatoes
- 2/3 of a cup tomato juice (passata)
- a pinch sugar
- a pinch of cinnamon or a cinnamon stick
- salt and freshly ground pepper

Method:

1. Start by heating a large frying pan over medium heat, pour in 2 tablespoons olive oil and sauté the onions, until soft. Season the chicken pieces with salt and pepper and add in the pan; fry the chicken breasts until lightly colored.
2. Remove the chicken pieces and the onions on a plate. In the same pan, add 2 tablespoons olive oil and sauté the orzo pasta. Add the tomato paste and continue sautéing. Pour in the tinned tomatoes, the tomato juice and a cup of warm water. Return the chicken pieces and onions in the pan, add a pinch of sugar, a pinch of cinnamon and season well with salt and pepper.
3. Turn the heat down to medium, place the lid on and cook for about 15 minutes, stirring occasionally, until the orzo

pasta is cooked. (Halfway through cooking time, check out if all of the liquid has been absorbed and add 1 cup of hot water into the pan).

4. Remove the pan from the stove, drizzle with olive oil and stir in the crumbled feta cheese.
5. Let the chicken with orzo rest for 5 minutes and serve while still warm.

Rolo Kima (Greek Meatloaf Stuffed with Eggs)

Serves: 8-10

Ingredients:

- 1.2 kg (40 ounces) minced beef
- 800g (30 ounces) minced pork
- 500-700 ml beef stock (2-3 cups)
- 100g (3.5 oz.) breadcrumbs
- 8-10 potatoes (cut into wedges)
- 4 medium-large eggs (hard-boiled)
- 3 cloves of garlic (mashed)
- 2 large red onions (grated)
- 2 tomatoes (grated)
- 1 tablespoon tomato paste
- 1/2 teaspoon powdered all-spice berries
- 1/2 cup olive oil
- salt and freshly ground pepper to taste

Method:

1. To prepare this impressive Greek meatloaf, add into a large bowl or basin the minced beef and pork along with the onions, garlic, tomatoes, the powdered all-spice berries, breadcrumbs and season well with salt and pepper. Mix thoroughly with your hands; it is important to knead the mix for at least 5-10 minutes so that all the ingredients combine and the meat absorbs all the wonderful flavors. Cover with some plastic wrap and let rest in the fridge for 20 minutes.
2. In the meantime, boil the eggs, for the stuffing and prepare the stock.
3. On a working surface line, a big piece of parchment paper and arrange half of the meat mixture as a base. Arrange

the hard-boiled eggs side by side along the length mixture; cover with the rest of the mixture and roll the parchment paper, forming a roll, so that it is curved down over the eggs in an arc.

4. Unroll carefully the meatloaf in a large, deep baking pan and add the potatoes (cut into wedges).
5. In a bowl, mix the stock, the tomato pastes and olive oil; pour 2/3 of the mixture over the meatloaf and potatoes.
6. Bake in preheated oven (at both top and bottom heating elements) at 180C, on the bottom grill of the oven for 1 hour 30 minutes. If the meatloaf starts getting colored to quickly, cover up with aluminum foil or lid. After an hour, check if all of the liquid has been absorbed and the pan appears to be getting dry and add the remaining stock mixture (warm), before the potatoes have fully browned.
7. Once the meatloaf is out of the oven let it rest for 15 minutes, to make it easier to slice. Slice into generous portions and pour over some of the delicious meat juices. Enjoy!

Lahanodolmades/Lahanodolmathes (Greek Stuffed Cabbage Rolls in Lemon Sauce)

Serves: 8-10

Ingredients:

For the cabbage rolls:

- 2 kg (70 ounces) cabbage
- 1kg (35 ounces) ground beef (mince)
- 90 ml rice (1/3 of a cup and 1 tablespoon)
- 2 medium-sized red onions (finely chopped)
- 2 medium-large egg whites
- 1 tablespoon chopped parsley
- 1 tablespoon chopped dill
- 1/3 of a cup olive oil
- salt and pepper

For the lemon sauce:

- 2 tablespoons butter
- 1/2 tablespoon flour
- 1 lemon (juiced, more if you like)
- 3/4 of a cup milk
- salt and pepper

Method:

1. Start by preparing the cabbage. Discard the outer leaves of the cabbage, open up carefully its leaves and wash thoroughly. In a large, deep pot, add some water and bring to the boil. Take some of the cabbage leaves and blanch them in the boiling water; parboiling the cabbage leaves before rolling them will make them softer and easier to roll. Remove with a slotted spoon and place on a clean working surface. Repeat with the rest of the

leaves. Once cool a little bit, remove the thick inner vein on the leaves and set aside (you will need them later).

2. Prepare the stuffing for the stuffed cabbage rolls. In a large bowl add the ground beef, the rice, the chopped onions, the parsley, the dill, the egg whites and season; knead the mixture well, squeezing the ingredients with your hands, so that the meat absorbs all the wonderful flavors.

3. Place one leaf on a flat surface (if it is too big, cut it in 2 or 3 smaller pieces), add a spoonful of the filling on the bottom center of the leaf; be careful not to overfill the rolls, as the rice will expand during cooking. Fold the lower section of the leaf over the filling towards the center; bring the two sides in towards the center and roll them up (not too tightly). Continue with the rest of the leaves and filling.

4. Layer the bottom of a large pot with the removed thick inner vein of the leaves (see step 1) and the smaller cabbage leaves that were too small for rolling. Lay on top the stuffed cabbage rolls, fold side down, and top in snugly packed layers. Season with salt and pepper and pour in the olive oil. Place an inverted plate on top to hold them down when cooking and pour in enough water to cover them. Place the lid on and bring to the boil. Turn the heat down and boil over medium heat for about 1 hour, until the cabbage is tender.

5. Drain the remaining water and set aside. Prepare the lemon sauce for the stuffed cabbage rolls. Melt the butter over medium heat, add the flour and whisk to form a paste. Pour in the lemon juice and ladle slowly the milk, whilst whisking. Pour in 3/4 of a cup of the drained liquid and whisk, until the sauce thickens a little bit.

6. Pour the sauce over the stuffed cabbage rolls and season well with freshly ground pepper. Enjoy!

Peinirli or Peynirli (Boat Shaped Greek Pizza)

Serves: 6-8

Ingredients:

- 400g (14 oz.) flour
- 400g (15 oz.) kasseri cheese or mix of mozzarella, edam, gouda or cheddar cheese
- 235g (8 oz.) milk at room temperature
- 30ml (3 tablespoons) olive oil
- 25g (1 oz.) butter
- 8g (2 1/2 tablespoons) dry yeast
- 2 teaspoons of salt
- 1 teaspoon of sugar
- 150g (5 oz.) bacon (optional)
- 1 green pepper (optional)

Method:

1. You can start by preparing the dough first. In the large bowl from an electric mixer add the milk (at room temperature), yeast and sugar and stir with a fork, so that the yeast dissolves completely. Into the same bowl, add the flour, butter, olive oil and salt. Use the dough hook to mix the ingredients in medium speed, for about 5-7 minutes. The dough for this Greek pizza recipe should be smooth and elastic and easy to roll
2. Coat lightly the dough with some olive oil, place the dough inside a large bowl and cover with plastic wrap. Let the dough sit in a warm place for at least 30 minutes, until it doubles its size.
3. Take the dough for your Greek pizza out of the bowl and split in 6 evenly sized portions. Stretch out the dough and shape in oval shaped, thin portions, like a pizza base.

4. For the topping for this Greek pizza recipe, grate the cheeses on top of the stretched-out dough and fold the dough corners to form its crust. Make sure you squeeze the ends so that the dough sticks together and doesn't unfold when baking. Fold the bottom edge first. Secure the edges by pressing them firmly or sealing them with a bit of water. Start folding the upper edge in the same way you did for the bottom. And lastly fold the two ends creating a boat-shaped pizza with raised edges. These will keep your ingredients in place.
5. Cut the bacon and peppers in little strips. Add the bacon and peppers on top, spreading them evenly.
6. Preheat oven at 180C and bake the peinirli for 20 minutes.
7. Remove from the oven and let the peynirli cool for a few minutes.

Beef Stifado (Greek Beef Stew)

Serves: 6-7

Ingredients:

- 1.5 kg (60 ounces) baby shallot onions (peeled)
- 1 kg (35 ounces) good-quality stewing beef (cut into portions)
- 3-4 allspice berries
- 3 tablespoons red wine vinegar
- 1 medium-large ripe tomato (roughly chopped)
- 1 teaspoon tomato purée
- 1 bay leaf
- 3/4 of a cup red wine
- 1/3 of a cup cognac
- 1/4 of a cup olive oil
- a pinch nutmeg
- salt and freshly ground pepper

Method:

1. Heat the oil in a medium-large saucepan, add the meat (in batches) and sauté, until browned on all sides. Do not add all the meat in the sauce pan, rather sauté in batches, so that the temperature of the oil remains high and the meat is sealed. When done, remove with a slotted spoon, place on a platter, cover and set aside.
2. Cut the baby shallot onions crosswise, add in the same oil used to browned the meat, turn down to medium heat and sauté until the onions have softened, but not browned (about 10 minutes).
3. Pour in the cognac, the wine and red wine vinegar, cover and let it simmer for about 3 minutes.
4. Pour the meat along with its juices to the saucepan, add the chopped tomato, tomato puree, bay leaf, allspice

berries and nutmeg. Bring to a boil, turn the heat down and simmer the beef stifado for 1 1/2 hours or until the beef is tender and the sauce has thickened. While the beef stifado is simmering, check if it needs some water; you don't want it to dry out. If it does, pour in half a cup of boiled water and stir. Towards the end of cooking time season well with salt and pepper to taste.

5. Serve beef stifado with pasta and grated cheese, or boiled new potatoes.

Gigantes Plaki (Greek Baked 'Giant' Beans)

Serves: 4-5

Ingredients:

- 500g (17 ounces) gigantes beans
- 400g (14 ounces) tinned chopped tomatoes or 600g (21 ounces) ripped fresh tomatoes (grated)
- 4-5 tablespoons parsley (finely chopped)
- 1 small clove of garlic
- 1 large onion (finely chopped)
- 1 teaspoon dried oregano
- 1/2 cup olive oil
- 1/2 tbsp celery (finely chopped)
- 1/2 cup of hot water
- salt and pepper to taste

Method:

1. Soak the gigantes beans overnight with plenty of water. Drain them into a colander and rinse.
2. Put the gigantes in a large pan with cold water, enough to cover them, add a pinch of sea salt and bring to a boil. Turn the heat down and simmer for 45 minutes, until tender but not cooked. Drain them in a colander and set aside.
3. In the meantime, pour into a large baking pan the olive oil, add the chopped onions, the whole garlic clove (peeled) and bake at 180C, until softened and slightly colored (approx. 15 minutes).
4. Turn the baking pan out of the oven; add the gigantes beans (drained), the celery, the parsley, ½ cup of hot water and season with salt and pepper. Put back in the oven and bake for 30 minutes.
5. Turn the baking tray out of the oven, blend the gigantes beans lightly with a wooden spoon and pour in the grated

tomatoes or plum tomatoes. Season with salt and pepper, add a pinch of oregano and bake the gigantes plaki further for 50-60 minutes at 180C, until the beans are soft and tender and the sauce thickens.

6. For an easier alternative, after soaking the gigantes beans overnight, drain and rinse them. Place in a large pan with enough water to cover them and bring to the boil. Boil for 5 minutes, drain them and place into a large baking pan, along with all of the ingredients, cover with some aluminum foil and bake at 180C for approx. 2 hours. The last 30 minutes, bake without the aluminium foil.

7. Serve while hot.

Moshari Kokkinisto (Greek Style Beef Stew in Tomato Sauce)

Serves: 6-7

Ingredients:

- 1 kg (35 ounces) of quality stewing beef
- 400g (14 ounces) spaghetti
- 100ml (2/5 of a cup) olive oil
- 4 ripe medium-large tomatoes (peeled and chopped)
- 2 small red onions (chopped)
- 2 cloves of garlic (chopped)
- 1-2 whole cloves, or a pinch grounded
- 1 teaspoon tomato paste, dissolved into a teacup of water
- 1 cinnamon stick
- a glass of red wine
- a pinch of sugar
- salt and pepper to taste
- grated cheese (kefalotyri) to serve

Method:

1. Cut the beef into pieces, approx. 100g/ 3.5 ounces each one. Wash the beef thoroughly and wipe with some paper towel. It is important to dry the meat well, in order to have a nice brown finish.
2. Heat a large, deep pot to high heat. After the pan is heated, pour in the oil along with the beef. Brown the pieces of beef on one side, without stirring and then brown them on the other side. Try not to overcrowd the bottom of the pan. Browning the beef is very important, when cooking a Greek beef stew, as it helps the meat remain juicy and tender.

3. Use a slotted spoon to remove the pieces of meat from the pot and place them on a plate.

4. For the sauce, add into the pot the chopped onions and turn the heat down. Sauté for 3 minutes, until softened. Stir in the garlic and sauté for 1 more minute. Pour in the red wine, turn the heat up and cook for 2 minutes, until it evaporates. Add the chopped tomatoes, the tomato paste (dissolved in a teacup of warm water), the cinnamon stick, the cloves, a pinch of sugar and salt and pepper.

5. The moment the sauce comes to the boil, add the beef and enough hot water to cover the 2/3 of the meat. When the sauce starts to bubble a lot, turn the heat down and half-cover with the lid (the sauce still has to bubble a little bit). Cook to medium-low heat, for about 1 1/2 hour, until the meat is tender and the sauce thickens, stirring occasionally.

6. If the meat is tender and cooked, but the sauce is not thick enough, remove the pieces of meat with a slotted spoon and boil the sauce alone to high heat, until it thickens. On the other hand, if the sauce becomes thick, before the meat is done, then add some warm water.

7. When done, boil the spaghetti into another pot, according to package instructions; drain and place in the pot, along with the sauce and the meat. Stir with a wooden spoon.

8. Serve the Greek beef stew with a drizzle of olive oil, sprinkle some grated cheese and enjoy over a glass of red wine.

Greek Bifteki (Burger) with Feta Cheese

Serves: 3-4

Ingredients:

- 500gr (18 ounces) minced beef or a combination of beef/lamb/pork
- 100g (3-4 ounces) feta cheese for topping
- 2 tablespoons parsley (chopped)
- 1-2 tablespoons salt
- 1 small-medium ripe tomato (grated)
- 1 red onion (grated)
- 1 clove of garlic (minced)
- 1 medium-large egg
- 1 teaspoon oregano
- 1 tablespoon olive oil
- 1 tablespoon red wine vinegar
- 1 teaspoon freshly ground pepper
- 1 tomato (sliced for topping)
- 2/3 cup breadcrumbs

Method:

1. Prepare a large bowl and Add the minced beef along with the rest of the ingredients and mix thoroughly with your hands. If the mixture is too sticky, add some more breadcrumbs (or some water if it is to dry), untill the mix is solid. If you have the time, it is better to knead the mixture for about 10 minutes, until all the ingredients combine. Alternatively, you can mix it using an electric mixer, with the dough hook at low speed.
2. When finish, put the mixture for the burgers (bifteki) in the fridge to rest for about 10 minutes, while preheating the oven to 200C.

3. Knead the mixture in flat round burgers. Place the biftekia on a large baking tray and cook in the oven for 18 minutes, flipping the burgers, mid-through cooking time. Top each bifteki with a slice of tomato and a small block of feta cheese and bake further for 7 minutes.
4. Serve while still hot with a drizzle of extra virgin olive oil and sprinkle a pinch of dried oregano.

Bakaliaros Skordalia (Cod Fritters with Garlic Potato Puree)

Serves: 5-6

Ingredients:

- 1-1.2kg (40 ounces) of salted cod
- 500g (18 ounces) water
- 500g (18 ounces) all-purpose flour, plus some extra for dredging
- 330ml beer (1 and 1/3 cups)
- 10g dry yeast (3 and 1/2 tablespoon)
- vegetable oil for frying
- a pinch of salt

For the sauce (Skordalia):

- 1 kg (35 ounces) potatoes (boiled)
- 4 cloves of garlic
- 1/2 cup of milk
- 1/2 cup of olive oil
- 1/3 cup of red wine vinegar or juice of 2 lemons
- salt to taste

Method:

1. To prepare the cod fritters, it is very important to leach the cod fish from the salt. To do that, soak the cod in water and put in the fridge. Leave it for 2-3 days and change the water 3 times a day. If you like you can buy some fresh cod fish and skip this procedure.
2. When finish, dry well the fish with paper towel and remove all the bones. Cut into small bites, 4-5 cm.
3. To prepare the batter for the cod fritters add into a bowl the beer, the water and the yeast and mix with a whisk,

until the yeast is dissolved. Add the rest of the ingredients and whisk, until the batter is smooth.

4. Into a deep-frying pan, heat the oil to high heat. Add some four into a bowl. Take one piece of cod and dredge into the flour, shaking it to remove the excess flour and then deep it into the batter, flipping it on all sides. Using a spoon remove the cod from the batter and put it slowly into the hot oil. Dip the spoon into some water and repeat with the rest of the pieces. Deep fry the cod fritters flipping them with allotted spoon, until nicely colored on all sides. Remove the cod fritters from the pan and place on some kitchen paper to drain. (Fry the cod fritters in batches, so that the surface of the pan is comfortably filled.)

5. Serve with creamy traditional Greek skordalia (garlic potato puree) and pita breads.

Tigania

Serves: 5-6

Ingredients:

- 1 kg (35 ounces) pork
- 200g (7 ounces) sausages (sliced)
- 2 peppers (sliced into strips)
- 1 glass of dry white wine
- 1 glass of tsipouro (Greek drink)
- 1 tablespoon mustard
- 1 teaspoon dry oregano
- 1 tablespoon paprika
- 1 onion (finely chopped)
- 1 cup of water
- 1/2 cup of olive oil
- salt and freshly ground pepper to taste

Method:

1. To start, wash the pork thoroughly over running water. Heat a large frying pan at high heat, pour in the olive oil and add the sausages and the pork. Sauté for 4-5 minutes, until nicely colored on all sides. Add the peppers and onions, and sauté for about 3-4 more minutes.
2. Pour in the tsipouro and season well with salt, pepper and a pinch of paprika.
3. Add a cup of water and 1 tablespoon of mustard into a bowl and blend. Add the water into the pan and stir. Cook until most of the juices have evaporated.
4. Add the wine, a good pinch of oregano and simmer with the lid on at medium heat for 6-7 minutes, until most of the juices have evaporated.

Kagiana or Strapatsada (Greek Fresh Tomato and Feta Egg Scramble)

Serves: 2-3

Ingredients:

- 1kg medium-large ripe tomatoes (grated)
- 6 medium-large eggs (beaten)
- 4-5 tablespoons olive oil
- a pinch of sugar
- salt and freshly ground pepper
- 100-150g/ 5 ounces feta cheese, crumbled (optional)

Method:

1. Prepare a large saucepan and add the olive oil and place on high heat. When the olive oil heats up, add the grated tomatoes, a pinch of sugar, season with salt and pepper and stir. In case you use feta cheese, be careful with the salt.
2. As soon as the tomato sauce comes to the boil, turn the heat down to medium and cook for about 10-15 minutes, until most of the juices have evaporated.
3. Pour in the beaten eggs and stir with a wooden spoon, so that the ingredients combine. Cook until the eggs are cooked. Feel free to add any kind of herbs you wish, like oregano, basil, mint or fresh dill.
4. Top with the feta cheese and serve, while still warm, with some crusted bread aside.

Kontosouvli (Spit Roasted BBQ pork)

Serves: 7-8

Ingredients:

For the marinade:

- 3 cups water
- 2 tablespoon olive oil
- 1 clove of garlic
- 1 teaspoon dry oregano
- 1 teaspoon paprika
- 1 tablespoon mustard
- 1/2 green pepper
- 1/2 onion
- salt and freshly ground pepper to taste

For the kontosouvli:

- 1-1.5 kg (40-50 ounces) medium-large potatoes (cut into wedges)
- 800g (28 ounces) pork shoulder (cut into large pieces)
- 1/2 green pepper (sliced)
- 1/2 onion (sliced)
- 1/2 tomato (sliced)
- one large wooden skewer

Method:

1. Start with the pork, cut into large pieces and place into a bowl (large enough to mingle easily with the marinade). Season with salt and pepper and add a pinch of oregano.
2. Add all the ingredients of the marinade into a blender and mix. Pour the mixture into the bowl with the pork

and blend. Cover with some aluminum foil and put the bowl in the fridge for 3 hours. Ideally leave it overnight.

3. Soak the wooden skewer into some water and thread the pieces of pork, comfortably, onto the skewer. In between the pieces of meat, add some sliced onion, pepper and tomato.

4. Place the kontosouvli on a large baking tray and add the potatoes, cut into wedges and season them with salt and pepper. Add 4 tbsps olive oil, 1/2 glass of water and sprinkle with a good pinch of oregano.

5. Cover with some aluminum foil and bake in preheated oven at 180C for 80 minutes. After 60 minutes, remove the aluminum foil and bake for another 20 minutes, until crunchy on the outside, tuning it upside down halftime through cooking time.

Tips:

- Use a piece of pork with some fat; this will make it even more delicious. While baking the pork, brush it with some olive oil and lemon juice; repeat 2-3 times. Personally, I prefer it, when the meat is a little burnt on the outside, as it reminds me of the traditional way of cooking it, over an open charcoal pit.

Kotopita (Greek Chicken Pie)

Serves: 6-8

Ingredients:

- 1 chicken, about 1kg (35 ounces)
- 60g (2 ounces) ham (finely chopped)
- 60g (2 ounces) bacon (chopped)
- 12 sheets of phyllo dough
- 7 tablespoons flour
- 3 red onions (sliced)
- 2 medium-large eggs
- 1 1/2 cup milk
- 1 cup kefalotyri, grated, or any hard yellow cheese
- 1 cup butter
- a pinch of nutmeg
- salt and freshly ground pepper to taste

Method:

1. Pour in enough water to cover the chicken and add the sliced onions and a good pinch of sea salt and bring to the boil. While the chicken boils, some white foam will probably surface on the water. Remove that foam with a slotted spoon. Put the lid on and boil for about 40 minutes, until the chicken is cooked through.
2. Remove the chicken from the pan and let it cool down for a while and keep the chicken stove aside. When it cools down, remove the skin and bones from the chicken and cut he meat into thin strips.
3. In the meantime, prepare the bechamel sauce. For the bechamel sauce, use a large pan and melt 5 tablespoons butter. Add 7 tablespoons of flour to the melted butter, whisking continuously to make a paste. Add the milk, warmed, in a steady steam, whisking continuously. Pour

in 1 1/2 cup of the chicken stove and continue whisking, until it slightly thickens. Remove from the heat and add the kefalotyri, the eggs, a pinch of nutmeg, salt and pepper and whisk. Add the chicken, along with the chopped ham and bacon and stir.

4. Melt the rest of the butter. Using a pastry brush, butter the bottom and sides of a baking tray (approx. 35*25 cm) and remove the phyllo roll from the plastic sleeve. You will use 8 sheets of phyllo for the bottom of the pie.

5. Begin by layering sheets one by one in the bottom of the tray, making sure to sprinkle each one thoroughly with the melted butter. Tip in the filling, smoothing the surface with a spatula. Fold the phyllo sheet flaps in over the chicken mixture. Add 4 sheets on top, sprinkling each sheet with melted butter. With a knife trim some of the excessive phyllo, if you like, and fold, rolling the rest on the edges. Brush the top with oil or butter and sprinkle with some water. Sprinkle with some white sesame seeds on top. Use a knife to make some holes on the top.

6. Bake in a preheated oven at 180C for 50-60 minutes, until the phyllo is crisp and golden. Let it cool down for a while before serving.

Kotopoulo Lemonato (Greek Lemon Chicken with Crispy Potatoes)

Serves: 4

Ingredients:

- 1 chicken (1.1kg/40 ounces), cut into 8 portions
- 1kg (35 ounces) medium potatoes (cut into wedges)
- 100g (4 ounces) feta cheese (cut into small cubes)
- 4-5 tablespoons extra virgin olive oil
- 3 medium lemons (juiced)
- 1 clove of garlic
- 1 teaspoon white wine vinegar
- 1 teaspoon peppercorns
- 1 teaspoon dry oregano
- freshly ground salt and pepper to taste

Method:

1. Start by cutting the chicken into 8 portions and wash thoroughly. Peel the garlic and rub on the chicken. Place on a large baking tray and season well with salt and pepper.
2. Cut the potatoes into wedges and place them between the chicken. Pour in some water, enough to cover half the chicken and add the lemon juice, the white wine vinegar, the olive oil, the chopped garlic and the peppercorns. Season with salt and pepper and add a good pinch of oregano. (Tip: sprinkle the potatoes with 1 tsp semolina for crispier results)
3. Cover with aluminum foil and bake in a preheated oven at 180C for 60-75 minutes in total. 50 minutes into the bake remove the aluminum foil and top the chicken with some feta cheese. Bake for another 15-20 minutes (the

remaining time), until your Greek lemon chicken is nicely colored and crispy on the outside.

4. This Greek lemon chicken is ideally served with a refreshing Greek feta salad and lots of sourdough bread aside to dig into all the delicious sauce!

Chapter Four: Greek Dessert Recipes

Samali (Greek Semolina cake with Mastic)

Serves: 2-3

Ingredients:

- 3-4 tablespoons butter (melted)
- 2 and 1/2 cups coarse semolina (or 1 1/2 coarse and 1 thin)
- 1 and 1/2 cup sugar
- 1 and 1/2 cup Greek yogurt
- 1 teaspoon baking powder
- 1 teaspoon baking soda
- 1/2 teaspoon ground mastic resin (you can buy it online in Australia, UK, US/CA)
- blanched almonds (garnish)

For the syrup:

- 2 and 1/2 cups sugar
- 1 and 1/2 cup water
- 1 lemon (cut in half)
- 1/2 tsp rose water (or vanilla extract or mastic or 1 cinnamon stick)

Method:

1. Start by using a blender to ground the masticha, along with a pinch of sugar and set aside. (Mastic will give Greek semolina cake its distinctive taste and amazing smell. But be careful not to add any more mastic than this samali recipe calls for, as it will leave a slightly bitter taste to your Greek semolina cake).

2. Put the yogurt in a bowl and add the baking soda. Blend to combine and set aside. In another bowl add the semolina, sugar, ground mastic and baking powder and blend with a spoon to combine. Add the yogurt mixture in the semolina mixture and whisk until the mixture is smooth and all the ingredients combine.

3. For this Greek semolina cake recipe (samali) you will need a large baking pan, approx. 38*28cm. Butter the bottom and sides of the pan and pour in the mixture. The mixture for this Greek semolina cake is a little bit tight (not liquid) so even out the surface of the samali using a wet spatula.

4. Cover the samali (Greek semolina cake) with a towel and let it rest for 3 hours.

5. Using a knife score the Greek semolina cake into little individual pieces and garnish with blanched almonds. Bake the samali in preheated oven at 180C for 35-40 minutes, until nicely coloured and cooked through.

6. In the meantime, prepare the syrup for the Greek semolina cake. In a small pot add all the ingredients for the syrup and bring to the boil. Let the syrup boil for 2-3 minutes, until the sugar was dissolved and the syrup has slightly thickened. Set aside to cool.

7. Turn the cake out of the oven and using a cooking brush, brush the top with the melted butter. Ladle slowly the cold syrup over the hot samali cake, allowing each ladle of syrup to be absorbed, before ladling again. Allow time for the syrup to be absorbed.

8. Let the samali cake cool down completely before serving.

Kourampiedes/Kourabiethes (Greek Christmas Butter Cookies)

Serves: 6-8

Ingredients:

- 1kg (35 ounces) icing sugar for powdering
- 450-500g (16-18 ounces) all-purpose flour (sifted)
- 250g (9 ounces) cow milk butter (room temperature)
- 100g (3.5 ounces) icing sugar
- 100g (3.5 ounces) almonds, whole or roughly chopped, with the peel
- 6g (1 1/2 teaspoon) baking powder
- 2 tablespoons ouzo (Greek drink)
- 1 teaspoon vanilla extract
- 1 tablespoon rose water

Method:

1. Preheat your oven at 200C. Place the almonds whole or roughly chopped (depending on whether you prefer the cookies to have whole or chopped almonds inside) on a baking tray and sprinkle with some water. Bake them for 7-8 minutes, being careful not to burn them.
2. Use an electric mixer, to mix the butter and the icing sugar (100g/3.5 ounces), for about 20 minutes, until the butter is creamy and fluffy, like whipped cream. (It is very important that the butter is at room temperature.) Add the vanilla extract, the rose water and the ouzo and blend; add the baked almonds and blend again.
3. In another bowl, blend the sifted flour and the baking powder. (It is very important to sift the flour, so that the cookies will become light and smooth.) Gradually add the flour into the butter mixture (from step 2) and work the

mixture with your hands, until the ingredients are combined and the dough is soft and easy to work. You will need 450-500g of flour, depending on the flour.

4. Preheat the oven to 200C; layer the bottom of 2 baking trays with parchment paper and form the kourampiedes. Roll 1-2 tbsps of the dough into a ball, place on the baking tray and push with your finger in the middle, to form a little dimple. Continue with the rest of the dough.

5. Place the baking trays with the kourampiedes in second and fourth grill of the oven and turn the heat down to 180C. Bake for approx. 20 minutes, until they have a very faint golden tint and are cooked through. Be careful not to overcook them. Leave them aside to cool down for a while. If you try to lift them, while still warm, they will break.

6. In a large bowl, add 500g/18 ounces of icing sugar and dip the kourampiedes (in batches) in the sugar, rolling them around, so that the sugar sticks on all sides. Place on one or two large platters. When done, sift the extra 500g/18 ounces icing sugar over the kourampiedes.

Galaktoboureko (Custard Pie With Phyllo)

Serves: 6-8

Ingredients:

For the filling:

- 6 cups milk
- 6 medium-large egg yolks
- 2 tablespoons unsalted butter
- 1 1/4 cups fine semolina (you can substitute farina)
- 1 tablespoon vanilla extract
- 1/2 cup sugar

For the phyllo:

- 1-pound phyllo pastry sheets
- 2 sticks unsalted butter (melted, for brushing phyllo)

For the syrup:

- 1 cup sugar
- 1 cup water
- 2-inch piece of lemon rind
- 2-inch piece of orange rind
- 1/2 lemon (juiced)

Method:

Make the filling:

1. In a big saucepan, heat the milk over medium-high heat until just boiling. Add the semolina and stir with a whisk. Lower the heat to medium-low.
2. Using a whisk, beat the egg yolks with the sugar in a bowl. Ladle a cup of the warmed milk into the egg mixture to

124

temper and then add the egg yolk mixture to the saucepan.

3. Continue to cook over medium-low heat until the cream starts to thicken, stirring continuously.
4. When the custard has thickened, remove from heat and stir in the vanilla extract and the butter. Set aside.
5. Unwrap the Phyllo
6. Carefully remove the phyllo roll from the plastic sleeve. Most packages come in 12x18 inch sheets when opened fully. Using a scissor or sharp knife, cut the sheets in half to make two stacks of 9x12 inch sheets. To prevent drying, cover one stack with wax paper and a damp paper towel while working with the other.
7. Preheat the oven to 350 F.

Assemble the Galaktoboureko:

1. Using a pastry brush, brush the bottom and sides of a 9x12 rectangular pan with melted butter. You will use approximately half the phyllo sheets for the bottom of the pastry. Begin by layering sheets one by one in the bottom of the pan, making sure to brush each one thoroughly with melted butter.
2. When you have almost layered half the sheets, drape two sheets of phyllo so that they extend half in the pan and half out of the pan horizontally. Add the custard in an even layer on top of the sheets, smoothing the surface with a spatula. Fold the phyllo sheet flaps in over the custard layer, then add the remaining sheets on top, brushing each sheet with melted butter.
3. Before baking, score the top layer of phyllo (making sure not to puncture the filling layer) to enable easier cutting of pieces later. (You can place the pan in the freezer for about 10 to 15 minutes to harden the top layers and then use a serrated knife.)
4. Bake in a preheated oven for 45 minutes or until the phyllo turns a deep golden color.

Prepare the syrup:

1. Combine the sugar and water in a saucepan and add the lemon peel and orange peel. Boil over medium-high heat for 10 to 15 minutes. Remove the lemon and orange peel and stir in the lemon juice. Remove from heat and set aside to cool.
2. Do not pour hot syrup over the hot custard. Allow both to cool to room temperature and then carefully ladle the syrup over the galaktoboureko and allow time for it to be absorbed.

Loukoumades (Delicious Lenten Greek Honey puffs recipe)

Serves: 4-5

Ingredients:

- 200g (7 oz.) self-rising flour
- 280g (9.8 oz.) water
- 50g (1.7 oz.) corn starch
- 9g (1 1/2 tablespoon) dry active yeast
- 1 tablespoon honey
- 1 teaspoon salt
- honey and chopped walnuts (garnish)

Method:

1. Start by dissolving the yeast in the water. Cover with plastic wrap and allow to rise for about 5 minutes, until it starts bubbling.
2. In another bowl add the flour, corn starch and salt and blend to combine. Add the flour mixture in the yeast mixture and pour in the honey. Whisk all the ingredients together, until the batter is smooth. Cover the bowl with plastic wrap and let the dough rise for about 30 minutes.
3. Into a medium sized frying pan pour enough vegetable oil to deep fry the loukoumades. Heat the oil to high heat (175-180C) until it begins to bubble. Test if the oil is hot enough by dipping in some of the dough. If it sizzles the oil is ready.
4. Take a handful of the dough in your palm and squeeze it out, between your thumb and index finger, onto a wet teaspoon. Then drop it in the oil and fry until golden. Repeat this procedure until the surface off the pan is comfortably filled. It is important to dip the spoon in a glass of water every time, so that the batter doesn't stick on it.

5. While being fried, use a slotted spoon to push the honey puffs into the oil and turn them around, until golden brown on all sides. Place the loukoumades on some kitchen paper to drain and repeat with the rest of the dough.

6. When done, place these delicious golden Greek honey puffs on a large platter, drizzle with (heated) honey and sprinkle with cinnamon and chopped walnuts. Enjoy!

Kataifi

Serves: 6-8

Ingredients:

- 450g (16 oz.) kataifi dough
- 250g (9 oz.) butter from cow's milk
- 250g (9 oz.) walnuts (roughly chopped)
- 1 teaspoon ground cinammon
- a pinch ground clove

For the syrup:

- 450g (16 oz.) sugar
- 330g (12 oz.) water
- peel of 1 lemon
- 1 cinnamon stick

Method:

1. Start by preparing the syrup. Add all the ingredients for the syrup into a small pot and bring to the boil. As soon as the sugar has dissolved, the syrup is ready. Leave the syrup aside to cool completely.
2. Prepare the filling for the Kataifi. In a blender add the walnuts, ground clove and cinnamon; pulse until the walnuts are roughly chopped (not powdered). Although the walnut filling is the most common, lots of kataifi recipes also add pistachios and almonds. So it's up to you to decide.
3. Melt the butter and with a cooking brush butter the bottom and sides of a baking pan. (approx. 26-28cm diameter)
4. Unroll the Kataifi dough from the plastic sleeve. Work the kataifi dough with your hands, tearing apart the shreds and gently spreading the strands out a bit if they

clump together, in order to get fluffy. Cover the Kataifi dough with a slightly damp towel.

5. Take one piece of the kataifi dough, and spread it on a working surface or on your palm. Drizzle with melted butter and place 1 teaspoon of the filling at one end. Roll it up tightly, folding inwards the sides, to form a small cylinder. Place the kataifi roll in the pan and brush with melted butter, using the cooking brush to shape it a little bit. Repeat with the rest of the kataifi dough and filling. Place the kataifi rolls the one next to the other, leaving no gaps between them and drizzle with a little bit more butter.

6. Bake the kataifi in preheated oven at 170-180C for about 1 hour (on the middle rack), until nicely coloured and crispy.

7. As soon as you turn the kataifi out of the oven, ladle slowly the 3/4 of the cold syrup over the for kataifi, enabling each ladle to be absorbed. Cover the pan with a towel and set aside for 10 minutes. Ladle the rest of the syrup over the kataifi and wait until absorbed.

8. Serve this delicious kataifi dessert with a full spoon of vanilla ice-cream. Enjoy!

Rizogalo (Greek Rice Pudding)

Serves: 1-2

Ingredients:

- 1200ml milk
- 100g (3.5 oz.) arborio rice
- 60g (2 oz.) sugar
- 1/2 teaspoon vanilla extract
- zest of an orange or lemon peel (optional)

Method:

1. To prepare this delicious Greek rice pudding, heat the milk and rice in a large heavy bottomed saucepan. Simmer over medium heat, stirring constantly, until it comes to just below boiling point. Reduce the heat to medium-low and gently cook, stirring occasionally, for 30-40 minutes until the pudding is thick and the rice is tender. (If you like to add some extra flavour to your Greek rice pudding, add some lemon peel or orange zest)
2. When preparing a Greek rice pudding, it is very important to simmer at low temperatures and to stir the mixture, so that the milk doesn't burn and the rizogalo doesn't stick on the bottom of the pan.
3. Remove the pan from the stove and add the sugar and the vanilla extract, stirring, until the sugar dissolves. (If the rizogalo needs to thicken a little bit more, dilute 1 tsp cornstarch in some water, add in the mixture and cook for a few more minutes.)
4. If you don't serve the Greek rice pudding right away, it will form a crust. A little trick to avoid that is to pour the mixture in a large bowl and place over a bowl filled with ice cubes. Then stir the mixture until cold. Spoon the rizogalo into individual bowls and store in the fridge.

5. Serve this traditional Greek rice pudding as a delicious dessert or mid-day snack with a sprinkle of cinnamon. Enjoy!

Trigona Panoramatos (Phyllo Triangle Pastries with Custard)

Serves: 8-10

Ingredients:

- 200g (7 ounces) butter (melted)
- 14-15 sheets phyllo dough

For the custard:

- 950g/33.5 ounces milk, divided in 700g/24 ounces and 250g/9.5 ounces
- 300g (10.5 ounces) sugar
- 250g (8.8 ounces) all-purpose flour
- 50g (1.8 ounces) butter (room temperature)
- 3-4 medium-large egg yolks
- 1 teaspoon vanilla extract
- 1 tablespoon icing sugar
- 1/3 of a cup heavy whipping cream (cold)

For the syrup:

- 500g (17.6 ounces) sugar
- 400g (14.1 ounces) water

Method:

1. To prepare these amazing dessert, start by making the syrup. In a pan add the sugar and water and bring to the boil; the syrup is ready, as soon as the sugar dissolves. Leave aside to cool down for a while.
2. Unroll the phyllo dough from the plastic sleeve and place on a working surface. Using a sharp knife cut the sheets of phyllo in three lanes (cut the shorter side in three lanes) and set aside. Lay one piece on the working surface

(shorter side facing you) and using a cooking brush drizzle with melted butter. Spread one more sheet on top and drizzle with some more butter. Fold one corner to form a triangle and continue folding the triangle upon itself, until the entire piece of phyllo is used. Cut the triangle in the middle to form two little triangles. Wrinkle some parchment paper into a little ball. Expand with your fingers the phyllo triangle to make an opening and place inside the paper ball. Continue with the rest phyllo sheets.

3. Line a large baking tray with parchment paper, place the phyllo triangles on top and brush them with melted butter. Bake in preheated oven at 160C for about 30 minutes, until nicely coloured.

4. As soon as you turn them out of the oven, remove the parchment paper from the inside of the phyllo triangles and dip them in the cold syrup, turning them sides; remove with a slotted spoon and set aside to cool down.

5. Prepare the custard for the pastries. In a pan add 700g/ 24 ounces milk, the sugar and vanilla extract and bring to the boil. In a bowl add 250g/ 9.5 ounces milk and the egg yolks; whisk to combine. Add the flour in the bowl and whisk to combine. As soon as the milk comes to the boil, remove from the heat and ladle slowly 1/3 of the milk into the flour mixture and whisk. Place the pan with the milk again on the stove and turn the heat down to medium. Add the flour mixture into the pan with the remaining warm milk; whisk continuously, until the mixture has thickened and is smooth and creamy. Remove the pan from the stove, add the butter and stir.

6. Pour the custard in a large tray, cover with some plastic wrap (the plastic wrarp should be touching the custard, so that it doesn't form a crust) and place in the fridge to cool.

7. Put the cold heavy cream into a mixer's bowl, add the sugar and beat into whipped cream. Remove the custard

from the fridge, add the whipped cream and fold gently to combine. Using a pastry bag, fill the triangles with custard and garnish chopped nuts. Enjoy!

Tiganites (Greek-style Pancakes with Honey and Walnuts)

Serves: 1-2

Ingredients:

- 2 cups all-purpose flour
- 2 cups of lukewarm water
- 1 teaspoon dry yeast
- 1 teaspoon sugar
- 1/2 teaspoon salt

To serve:

- 1/2 cup warm honey
- some chopped walnuts

Method:

1. Start by pouring the water and yeast in a large bowl; stir with a fork, so that the yeast dissolves completely. Into the same bowl, add the rest of the ingredients for the pancakes and whisk to form a smooth batter. Cover with some plastic wrap and leave aside for 15-20 minutes, until the batter starts to bubble.
2. Heat a nonstick large skillet or griddle pan over medium heat and pour in enough corn oil to cover the bottom of the pan (approx. 2 tablespoons).
3. Spoon 1-2 tablespoons of the batter (depending on how large you want them) in the hot oil. Don't overcrowd the pan; fry the pancakes in batches (3-4 at a time). Fry until nicely colored, flipping them sides; transfer to some kitchen paper, to absorb the oil and repeat with the rest.
4. Serve while still warm with a drizzle of warm honey and sprinkle with chopped walnuts.

Vasilopita Cake Recipe (Greek New Year's cake)

Serves: 6-8

Ingredients:

For the vasilopita:

- 750g (26.5 ounces) self-rising flour (sifted)
- 375g (13 ounces) butter
- 200g (7 ounces) yogurt (strained)
- 6 medium-large eggs (separate into yolks and whites)
- 3 cups sugar
- 1 teaspoon vanilla extract
- 1/2 cup orange juice
- a pinch of salt
- zest of 2 oranges

For the glaze:

- 3 cups icing sugar
- 3 tablespoons hot water or milk
- 1 teaspoon vanilla extract

Method:

1. Start by seperating the eggs into yolks and whites. Place the egg whites in the bowl of the electric mixer, along with a pinch of salt. Make sure your egg whites, bowl and whisk attachments are clean and free of any water. Whisk the egg whites until the mixture is very thick and glossy and a long trailing peak forms when the whisk is lifted (meringues). Place the mixture in a bowl and set aside.
2. Use the electric mixer, to mix the butter and sugar, for about 20 minutes, until the butter is creamy and fluffy,

like whipped cream. Add the egg yolks, one at a time, whilst mixing, allowing time for each one to be absorbed, before adding another. Pour in the orange juice, the vanilla extract, the orange zest, the yogurt and mix to combine. Add 1/3 of the sifted flour and blend, using a maryse spatula. Add 1/3 of the meringues and blend with light circular movements from the bottom up. Repeat with the rest of the flour and meringue (adding 1/3 of the flour and 1/3 meringue and then the remaining flour and meringue).

3. To bake the vasilopita, preheat the oven to 200C (both top and bottom heating elements on). Butter the bottom and sides of a round non-sticking cake tin (approx.32cm diameter) and pour in the mixture. Place the cake tin in the preheated oven, on the lower rack, turn the heat down to 175C and bake for 50-60 minutes, until nicely colored and cooked through. Check if the vasilopita is ready, by sticking in the middle of the cake a wooden skewer or toothpick. If it comes out clean, then the cake is ready.

4. Let the vasilopita cool down (otherwise it will break) and invert the pan on a plate. Wrap a coin with aluminum foil and stick it in the cake. Invert the vasilopita on a serving platter.

5. Prepare the glaze for the vasilopita. In a large bowl add all the ingredients and blend with a spatula to combine, until the glaze is smooth and glossy. Add a little bit more hot water, if needed (the glaze should be like a thin cream). Top the vasilopita with the glaze and even out with a spatula. Don't forget to carve the number of the year on top of the glaze! Enjoy!

Conclusion

I would like to thank you once again for purchasing this book.

Greek cuisine is very diverse in that a certain recipe may have variations within a different part of Greece. To get that distinct Greek flavor and to add authenticity to the taste of your dish, I suggest that you use products imported from Greece, that are readily available in grocery stores – such as Greek olive oil for example.

This book will help you create and plan meals that will give you a true taste of Greece. Impress your family and friends by planning a Greek-themed dinner party and be assured that we will have you covered.

But always remember that great food starts with great ingredients. Do not be afraid to season your dish, and always taste as you cook to balance out the flavors. Cooking is a learning process, and you become a better cook each time you remake the dish that you want to master. This book will help you achieve that.

Thank you and all the best.

Other Books by Grizzly Publishing

"Jamaican Cookbook: Traditional Jamaican Recipes Made Easy"

https://www.amazon.com/dp/B07B68KL8D

"Brazilian Instant Pot Cookbook: Delicious Pressure Cooked Meals Made Fast and Easy"

https://www.amazon.com/dp/B078XBYP89

"Norwegian Cookbook: Traditional Scandinavian Recipes Made Easy"

https://www.amazon.com/dp/B079M2W223

"Casserole Cookbook: Delicious Casserole Recipes From Around The World"

https://www.amazon.com/dp/B07B6GV61Q

Made in the USA
Monee, IL
18 January 2021